An Interviewee's Guide To F&B Service

2,150 QUESTIONS AND ANSWERS ON F&B SERVICE

VARGHESE JOHNSON

Notion Press Media Pvt Ltd

No. 50, Chettiyar Agaram Main Road,
Vanagaram, Chennai, Tamil Nadu – 600 095

First Published by Notion Press 2021
Copyright © Varghese Johnson 2021
All Rights Reserved.

ISBN 978-1-63940-413-1

Contents

Foreword

I am delighted to write this foreword, not only because Prof. Varghese Johnson has been a student, colleague and above all a friend for more than twenty years, but also because I believe deeply in the educative value of the book for all students of hotel and hospitality management, especially those interested in Food and Beverage Service. I also believe that Food and Beverage professionals at every level and stage of their career can enrich and strengthen their knowledge by reading this book. The book 'An Interviewee's Guide to F&B Service' is a reflection of the deep understanding of the subject that Prof. Varghese has as well as the passion with which he teaches his students. The 2150 questions and answers arranged in five chapters of the book will guide the students through the subject and enable them to face interviews and viva-voce with confidence. I recommend this as a must have book for all aspiring Food and Beverage executives.

– Dr. Anil Kumar

Registrar
Srinivas University
Mangalore

Preface

'An Interviewee's Guide to F&B Service' is my fourth book related to F&B Service. It's been my long time wish to write a book which would help F&B aspirants to strengthen their F&B knowledge and confidently face their interviews. So, after a span of 6 long years I am back. The inspiration to come up with such a topic was the worried frenzy seen in my students past and present, as they prepare for their job interviews. The objective is to help hospitality and hotel management students to prepare well and appear for F&B related interviews. I firmly believe that knowledge is something which will boost one's confidence. No matter how big or small is information pertaining to a subject, it's still knowledge enhancement. The questions and answers given in the book will surely enable the students to strengthen their subject knowledge and could be used for conducting F&B related quizzes and activities.

I am greatly thankful to God for his steadfast love and endless blessings. I thank my parents and brother for their constant encouragement and tremendous support. My wife, Sonia has always been inspirational and has always encouraged me in doing something better. I thank her for the editorial work carried out for this venture. Love to Ann, my daughter for her unconditional love and patience.

I am also grateful to Dr. Anil Kumar, Registrar, Srinivas University, Mangalore for his help and guidance through the preparation of this book and for honouring me by writing the foreword for this book.

Happy reading!

Pala
01-06-2021   – **Varghese Johnson**

CHAPTER-1

Finding Yourself

FINDING YOURSELF

EVERYTHING IS POSSIBLE IF YOU PUT YOUR MIND IN WHAT YOU DO.

THINK!

STEP 1   ARE YOU REALLY INTERESTED IN HAVING A CAREER IN F&B SERVICE?

STEP 2   WHAT ARE YOUR CAREER OBJECTIVES?

STEP 3   WHAT DO YOU FEEL IS YOUR STRENGTH IN F&B SERVICE? FOOD OR BEVERAGES?

STEP 4   WHERE YOU SEE YOURSELF AFTER TEN YEARS?

STEP 5   HAVE FAITH IN GOD. BE CONFIDENT.

FOUR KEYS TO UNLOCK THE WORLD TO SUCCESS

CONFIDENCE – Grooming, excellent communication skills, subject knowledge and right attitude.

WISDOM – Gain it through relentless practice.

KNOWLEDGE – Experience, observation, learning……There is no end to it.

SELF-MOTIVATION – Be a good motivator. You are the best motivator for yourself.

CHAPTER-2

The Basics

Section no.	Sub-heading	Questions
2.1	General	52
2.2	Catering	15
2.3	Operational equipment	100
2.4	Food and Beverage Outlets	35
2.5	Food and Beverage Staff	20
2.6	Menu	30
2.7	Food and Beverage Service Terminology	50 terms

2.1 General

1) Define Hospitality.

Hospitality can be defined as the friendly reception and treatment extended to clients.

2) From which word did the term 'hospitality' originate?

The word 'hospitality' originated from the Latin word 'hospes'.

3) Which fruit is regarded as the 'symbol of hospitality' universally?

Pineapple.

4) Why is Pineapple regarded as the 'symbol of hospitality'?

There existed a tradition among Americans during the early colonial days that if a pineapple fruit is displayed either on the front gates of the house or as a centerpiece on a dining table, it denoted that the host feels very happy in receiving and treating their visitors.

5) How is hospitality and boar's head related?

During ancient days, boar's head was used as a symbol of hospitality which denoted that the host is willing to feed the guests well.

6) What is a Hotel?

British Law defines **a 'Hotel'** or 'Inn' as 'a **place where a bonafide** traveller can receive food and shelter, provided he is in a position to pay for it and is in a fit condition to be received'.

7) What is the tagline of Indian tourism?

'Athithi Devo Bhava'.

8) What does the term 'Athithi Devo Bhava' mean?

Guest is God.

9) Who is regarded as the 'Father of Indian Hospitality industry'?

Mohan Singh Oberoi.

10) What's the title bestowed upon Mr. Oberoi by the British government for his contributions?

Rai Bahadur.

11) Who initiated 'Oberoi group of hotels'?

Mohan Singh Oberoi.

12) Who started 'Taj group of hotels'?

Jamsetji Nusserwanji Tata.

13) Name the founder of 'Leela group of hotels.'

Captain C.P Krishnan Nair. (Captain Chittarath Poovakkatt Krishnan Nair).

14) Which was the first Indian hotel, constructed by an Indian for Indians with international standards?

The Taj Mahal Palace Hotel, Mumbai.

15) Who was the 'Chef to kings and king of chefs'?

Georges-Auguste Escoffier.

16) Who is considered as the 'Hotelier to kings' and 'king of hoteliers'?

César Ritz.

17) Who is regarded as the first lady of Indian hospitality?

Thangam Philip

18) Who is regarded as the 'Father of Industrial catering'?

Robert Owen.

19) Name India's first trademarked building.

The Taj Mahal Palace Hotel, Mumbai.

20) Name the department that is held responsible for the service of food and beverages in a hotel.

F&B Service.

21) Name the restaurants located in Eiffel tower.

58 Tour Eiffel and Le Joules Verne.

22) Why the restaurant located in the first floor of Eiffel tower is named as '58 Tour Eiffel'?

The restaurant is located 57 metres from the ground to which 1 metre could be added of the kitchen range.

23) Name the restaurant located in Navi Mumbai, India that features chain conveyors through which one's food orders could be placed.

Bruciato Food Factory (BFF), Airoli.

24) What is so unique about 'Kaidi Kitchen' located in Mylapore, Chennai?

'Kaidi Kitchen' located in Chennai is a dining restaurant which revolves around prison theme (staff dressed themselves as waiters and jailors) that serves Indian, Mexican, Italian and Mongolian cuisine.

25) Is there any robot themed restaurant in India?

Yes, a robot themed restaurant is located in Chennai at Kamraj Nagar. In this restaurant, the guest can place the order through an ipad placed on the table. Food will be served to the guest by the robots.

26) What is the unique feature of 'Dans Le Noir' restaurant located in Paris?

'Dans Le Noir' restaurant located in Paris offers the guest a dining experience in darkness. The guests are served by visually impaired waiters.

27) What is 'Tokyo Snake Centre'?

'Tokyo Snake Centre' opened in 2015 is the name of a café (snack shop) which offers the guest food and beverages along with a non-poisonous snake in a glass box. It is located in Harajuku, Tokyo.

28) Name India's first cat café.

CCS also known as Cat Café Studio, Mumbai is India's first cat cafe.

29) Name the Indian restaurant situated in a graveyard.

New Lucky Restaurant in the La Darwaza area of Ahmedabad is situated in a graveyard.

30) Which is the oldest restaurant in the world?

Sobrino de Botin (opened in 1725) located in Madrid, Spain.

31) Name the largest restaurant in the world.

Bawabet Dimashq, a family owned restaurant in Damascus, Syria which was opened in 2002.

32) Name the first toilet themed restaurant in India.

Nature's Toilet Café located in Ahmadabad.

33) Which is India's first domestic luxury cruise liner?

Angriya.

34) Name the green house restaurant located in Amsterdam which serves vegetables and fruit based dishes.

Restaurant De Kas

35) Which was India's first touch table restaurant?

Touche Touch Table Diner Bar, Indiranagar, Bangalore.

36) Expand FHRAI.

FHRAI stands For Federation of Hotel and Restaurants Association of India.

37) What does TAAI stand for?

TAAI stands for the Travel Agents Association of India.

38) Expand NRAI.

National Restaurant Association of India.

39) From which language the word 'Namaste' is derived from?

The word 'Namaste' is derived from Sanskrit language by joining two words-'Namas' (means 'bow') and 'te' (means 'to you'). The spiritual meaning of Namaste being 'I bow to the divine in you.'

40) What is the symbolism of 'Namaste' (folding hands together)?

It is done to show due respect, but when hands and fingers combines together, it triggers our pressure points located in our eyes, ears and mind that enables us to remember that person for a longer time.

41) Why the practice of sitting on floor and consuming food is still followed?

The physical activity of bending spine will improve the blood circulation and metabolism.

This habit also aids in digestion and enable a person to avoid over eating.

42) Why water is sprinkled on banana leaves before serving food?

It is regarded as an act of purification.

43) What is the purpose of serving food on banana leaves?

'Polyphenols' (an antioxidant) which is present on banana leaves has the power to reduce diabetes, cancer and cardiovascular related diseases. When food is served on banana leaves, the integration releases nutrients that aids in digestion too.

44) Why the practice of eating food with one's hand is very common in India?

Indians believe that while having food with fingers, the nerves at the end of finger tips sends signal to the stomach which enhances the overall meal experience. As per Ayurveda, using five fingers stimulates the five elements and enables the digestives juices to run. Vedas say that this practice increases the circulation of blood.

45) Name the largest coffee house chain in the world.

Starbucks. As of 2019, Starbucks has more than 30,000 outlets around the globe.

46) Which coffee chain has twin-tailed mermaid (Siren) as its logo?

Starbucks.

47) Why most of the tables in Starbucks outlets are round in shape?

Starbucks believes in the theory "round table makes people feel less lonely."

48) What was a burger originally called as?

A burger was originally called as 'Hamburg steak'.

49) Which meat is traditionally used in hamburger?

Beef.

50) What are the accompaniments of Hamburger?

French fries, Potato wedges, Tomato ketchup, Mustard and Spicy pickles.

51) Name the hamburger chain restaurant that sells a product named 'Big Mac.'

McDonald's.

52) Name the hamburger chain restaurant that sells a product named 'The Whopper.'

Burger King.

2.2 Catering

1) What is Catering?

Catering is the activity of providing food and beverage for events.

2) Name two different types of catering

On premises and Off premises catering.

3) What is On premises catering?

On premises catering is a type of catering in which the guests are catered on the premises itself. Example is a banquet function happening in the hotel.

4) What is Off premises catering?

A type of catering where the guests are catered away from the premises. The food might be prepared in the hotel but served to the guests outside the hotel (according to the wish of the host).Example is an ODC scheduled outside the hotel.

5) Give few basic differences between On- premises and Off-premises catering

On- premises catering	Off- premises catering
Happens within the premises	Happens outside the premises
Transportation of food, beverages, banquet staff, equipment are not involved	Transportation of food, beverages, banquet staff, equipment are involved
Space and location constraints exists	No Space and location constraints
Sufficient electrical power, water and working space	Invariably lack sufficient electrical power, water and working space
Example is catering done in a banquet hall of a hotel	Example include Outdoor catering (ODC)

6) Define Function catering

Function catering can be defined as the service of food and beverages at a specific time, for a given number of people, to an agreed menu and price.

7) Give examples for function catering

Weddings, Social gatherings, Conferences, Meetings, Seminars etc. are few examples of function catering.

8) Which are the different types of catering sectors?

Commercial catering sector and Welfare catering sector.

9) What is Commercial catering sector?

Commercial catering sector is a kind of catering sector which focuses on attaining maximum profit by satisfying the everyday needs of the customers.

10) Give few examples for commercial catering units

Hotels, Restaurants, Pubs, Bars, Fast food outlets etc.

11) What is Welfare catering sector?

This sector of catering offers food and beverages for a reasonable rate with less profit or no profit. Welfare catering is seen in old age homes, prisons, hostels and destitute homes.

12) What is Transport catering?

Transport catering is serving/selling food and beverages to large number of customers who are travelling from one place to the other.

13) What is Club catering?

Club catering refers to the provision of food and beverages to a restricted member clientele.

14) What is Mobile catering?

It's a type of catering which involves either a vehicle or cart.

15) What is Food truck catering?

Food truck catering is catering to the food and beverage needs of the customers in a food truck.

2.3 Operating Equipment

1) What is Operating equipment?

Operating equipment is the equipment used in food and beverage outlets for its day to day operations.

2) Give few examples for operating equipment

Joint knife, Fish fork, AP spoon, Joint plate, Tea cup, Napkins, Restaurant table are examples for operating equipment.

3) Classify operating equipment

Tableware, Glassware, Crockery, Silverware, Linen, Furniture, Trolley, Special equipments etc.

4) What is Tableware?

Tableware includes a set of wares or articles set on a table for a meal. It's a term that covers cutlery, flatware, crockery, silverware and hollowware.

5) What is Dinnerware?

Dinnerware features different plates, bowls, saucers, platters etc…..all required for having a meal.

6) What is Flatware?

Flatware is a category of operating equipment which includes forks and spoons in all various sizes.

7) Give five examples for flatware

Soup spoon, AP spoon, Sweet spoon, Joint fork and Fish fork.

8) What is Cutlery?

Cutlery is a type of operating equipment that includes all types of knives and other cutting implements used by the guest to have a meal.

9) Give five examples for cutlery

Joint knife, AP knife, Cheese knife, Steak knife and Butter knife.

10) Mention few brand names for flatware and cutlery.

Venus, Kishco, Lenox, Knork, Wayfair etc.

11) What is the pointed part of a fork called?

Prongs/Tines.

12) How many prongs are there in a standard fork?

4 prongs.

13) How many prongs are there in an oyster fork?

3 prongs.

14) Why the fish fork is designed so?

It enables its user to easily separate the bones and flesh of a fish.

15) Why some cheese knives have holes in them?

This design enables the person to move the knife freely and saves the blade from sticking to the cheese while cutting cheese.

16) What is the purpose of prongs seen at the end of a cheese knife?

It is used for serving cheese.

17) What is a soup ladle?

Soup ladle is used for serving soup from soup tureen into soup bowls/plates.

18) What is Holloware?

Holloware, either made of silver or stainless steel is operating equipment which is mostly hollow from the top with a flat base.

19) Give five examples for holloware.

Soup tureen, Chafing dish, Water jug, Tea pot and Soup bowl.

20) What is a soup tureen?

Soup tureen is a ceramic hollowware used to serve soup for guests.

21) What is Glassware?

Glassware is a broad term used for various types of glasses that are used in various F&B outlets for the purpose of drinking potable drinks.

22) Give names of three glassware.

Tom Collins glass, High ball glass and Old fashioned glass.

23) Name any two raw materials used for making glassware.

Silver and soda ash.

24) What are the different parts of glassware?

There are mainly three parts for a glassware-Base (Foot), Stem and Bowl. A glass might have one, two or all the three of these parts.

25) What are the different types of glassware?

They are stemware, tumbler, mug and footed glassware.

26) What is Stemware?

A type of glassware best identified by its thinner stem that supports the bowl.

27) Mention five examples for stemware

Cocktail glass, Margarita glass, Red wine glass, White wine glass and Champagne saucer.

28) What is Tumbler?

Tumbler is a straight sided glass with a flat, stable bottom.

29) Give examples for tumblers.

Old fashioned glass, Tom Collins glass, High ball glass, Pilsner glass etc.

30) What is Stein/Mug?

Stein is large heavy glass with a side handle.

31) Give two examples for steins.

Beer mug and Irish coffee mug.

32) What is Footed glassware?

This glassware is a combination of tumbler and stemware. The bowl sits directly on its base.

33) Give two examples for footed glassware.

Brandy snifter and Hurricane glassware.

34) Mention few brand names for glassware.

Waterford, Ocean, Yera, Lyra, Luminarc, Cello etc.

35) Give the names and capacity of various glassware used in F&B outlets.

Name of the glassware	Capacity
AP/All Purpose wine glass	6-10 oz.(ounce)
Beer Boot glass	Many standard sizes-1 oz-2 L
Beer Mug/Beer Tankard	12 -16 oz.
Beer Goblet	14 oz.
Brandy snifter/Brandy balloon	5 - 8 oz.
Caballito glass	1-2 oz.
Champagne flute	7 - 10 oz.
Champagne saucer	6 oz.
Champagne tulip	9 oz.
Cocktail glass	4 -6 oz.
Collins/Tom Collins glass	12 -16 oz.
Copita Sherry glass	6 oz.
Franziskaner beer glass	12-20 oz.
High ball glass	8-12 oz.
Hurricane glass	15 oz.
Irish coffee glass	8 - 10 oz.
Margarita glass	12 oz.
Mini Pilsner beer glass	8-12 oz.
Old fashioned/Rock glass	8-12 oz.
Paris goblet	6-10 oz.

Pilsner beer glass	12-20 oz.
Pint /Becker/Nonic/Tumbler glass	2 standard sizes-16 oz. and 20 oz.
Pony Tumbler/Juice glass	5 oz.
Port wine glass	6½ oz.
Pousse café glass	6 oz.
Punch bowl	1-5 gal
Red wine glass	8 - 10 oz.
Rolly Polly glass	8 - 10 oz.
Sherry glass	2-6 oz.
Shot/Tequila Shot glass	1.5 oz.
Soda fountain glass	10-15 oz.
Sundae glass	15 oz.
Water goblet	8-10 oz.
Weizen beer glass	12-15 oz.
White wine glass	6 -8 oz.

36) What is Silverware?

Silverware is a term used to describe cutlery, flatware and hollowware that are either made of stainless steel or EPNS.

37) What is EPNS?

Electro Plated Nickel Silver. Equipment which is of EPNS grade usually has a copper-zinc and nickel alloy base which is highly polished with silver of varying thickness to give a very rich look of silver.

38) What is a Salver?

A salver is a type of operating equipment used in a restaurant by F&B staff. It's used to carry food and beverages to the guest's table and is also used to carry small operating equipment.

39) What is the standard size of a tray used in catering establishments?

18 ×13 ½ inches.

40) What is Crockery?

Crockery is a term used to denote different plates, bowls, cups and dishes used on a table used to serve food. They are normally made of clay and are found to be more heat resistant, but are easily fragile. Earthenware and Chinaware fall under this category.

41) Mention few brands of crockery

La Opala, Larah, Korin, Servewell, Corelle etc.

42) Give examples for crockery with its sizes.

Name of crockery	*Size*
B&B plate (Side plate)	15 cm (6 inches) diameter
Sweet plate	18 cm (7 inches) diameter
Fish plate (Half plate)	20 cm (8 inches) diameter
Soup plate	20 cm (8 inches) diameter
Joint plate	25 cm (10 inches) diameter
Cereal bowl	13 cm (5 inches) diameter
Consommé cup	300-400 ml
Soup bowl	240-360 ml
Breakfast cup	230-280 ml
Coffee cup	95 ml
Tea cup	190 ml

43) What does the term 'demi tasse' mean?

It means 'half cup'.

44) What is Earthenware?

Earthenware is white and porous clay which is fired at low temperature.

45) What is Stoneware?

Stoneware is hard clay which is fired at high temperature that results in sturdy and chip resistant material that can be used for various purposes.

46) Why is finished stoneware termed as 'vitreous'?

Stoneware is termed as vitreous because the finished product it has a distinct look of glass. The term 'vitreous' means 'like glass'.

47) List three differences between earthenware and stoneware.

Earthenware	*Stoneware*
More porous in nature than stoneware	Less porous in nature than earthenware
Less harder than earthenware	More harder than earthenware
Matures at lower temperature	Matures at higher temperature

48) What is Chinaware?

Chinaware, originally from China is a kind of tableware made of china clay. It is hard, often white in colour with a good glaze.

49) What is Porcelain?

Porcelain is a type of ceramic material that is manufactured by using raw materials which is heated in a kiln (a kind of oven) at very high temperature. Porcelain makes use of clay in the form of kaolin.

50) Mention few raw materials used to make Porcelain.

Kaolin, Bone ash, Quartz, Feldspar etc.

51) What is Kaolin?

Kaolin is a type of clay and is the primary material from which porcelain is made.

52) What is Melamine?

Melamine is a type of organic compound commonly used as a dinnerware. It is widely used in many catering establishments since it can withstand heat to a larger extent and at the same time is more durable than chinaware.

53) What is Bone china?

Bone china is chip resistant porcelain made from mixture of bones and kaolin.

54) What is Hotel china?

Hotel china is a type of chinaware widely used in catering establishments since it is heavy and crack resistant.

55) What is a Sideboard?

Sideboard is a type of furniture or an operating equipment used mainly in restaurants to support the F&B service staff. This furniture contains all the tableware items that are required for proper functioning of the restaurant. Dummy waiter is also used as a landing table for the dishes picked up from the kitchen enroute to the table.

56) Which are the other terms used for sideboard?

Étagère, Dummy waiter, Service console and Side station.

57) What is a Booster/Booster station?

Booster is a serving stand /cabinet which is mostly seen in the middle of a fine dining restaurant. This is often equipped with a hot plate and refrigerator.

58) What is Dumb waiter?

Dumb waiter is a type of small elevator or lift seen in building and is used to carry food from one floor to the other.

59) What is Restaurant linen?

Linen used in Restaurant for various purposes.

60) Give few examples for linen used in Restaurant

Restaurant uses various linen items like Table cloths, Baize cloths, Napperons, Napkins and Placemats.

61) What are the different sizes of the table cloth used in a restaurant?

It varies according to the size of the table.

Types of table	Table size	Tablecloth size
Square	A table of 76 cm^2	137 cm x137 cm
	A table of 1 m^2	183x183 cm
Rectangular	137x76 cm	183 x137 cm
Round	1m (dia.)	184 cm (dia.)

62) What is a baize cloth?

A kind of cloth fixed on table tops for holding the table cloths intact.

63) What is Napperon/Slip cloth?

Napperon is used to safe guard the table cloth from spillages and dirt. It reduces the number of tablecloths used on a table daily.

64) What is the size of Napperon/Slip cloth?

Slip cloth is found in different dimensions but usually measure 1m (3 ft) square.

65) What is the purpose of napkin in a restaurant?

Napkins are used for making napkin folding and are placed in the centre of a cover. The guests use it to dab their lips while having a meal.

66) What is the size of a napkin?

The size of a cloth napkin is 46-50 cm.

67) What's the French word for Napkin?

Serviette.

68) Give the names of few classic napkin folds.

Bishop's Maitre, The Wave, French lilly fold, The Breakfast fold etc.

69) What is a Napkin ring?

A ring used to hold the guest napkin especially when they are not in use.

70) What is Napkin holder?

Napkin folder is an equipment used to hold paper napkins on a table. It can either be made of highly polished stainless steel, wood or fibre.

71) What is Cocktail napkin?

It's a small cloth napkin provided to the guest along with the cocktails or other drinks in a bar and is used by the guest to dab his mouth. It's not seen in bars these days.

72) What is the size of cocktail napkin?

The size of cocktail napkin is generally 6"×6".

73) What is Waiter's cloth better known as?

Damask.

74) What's the normal size of damask?

The normal size is 18"x 18".

75) What is a Table runner?

A Table runner is a type of linen used to cover the middle part of the table. It 'runs' from one end of the table to the other.

76) What is the other term used for Table runner?

Deco-mat.

77) What are Table skirts?

Table skirts, also known as buffet cloths are used to cover buffet tables.

78) What are buffet tables?

These are long tables meant for buffets.

79) What are the common types of banquet tables used in various banquet functions?

Round, Square, Rectangular, Crescent, Half moon or half round shaped tables.

80) What is the size of a restaurant chair?

It's normally 3 feet from the ground to the top.

81) What is a bar stool?

Bar stool is a type of seating seen in bars, designed specifically for high eating and drinking surfaces, with long legs which elevate the seat so that a patron can sit in comfort.

82) What is the size of bar stool?

Most bar stools are around 30 inches (76 centimeters) in height.

83) Why bar stools comes without backrest?

It gives an indication to the bartender when the guest is drunk and it saves space when not in use (one can tuck it easily under the counter).

84) What is a trolley?

A moveable table with castors is a trolley.

85) Name few trolleys seen in F&B outlets.

Gueridon trolley, Room Service trolley, Bussing trolley, Hors-d'oeuvre trolley and Cheese trolley.

86) What are bar equipment?

Bar equipment are those equipment used in a bar by the bar staff.

87) Give examples for bar equipment.

Cocktail shaker, peg measure, bar spoon, bar mat, speed opener, ice chisel etc.

88) What is Marmite?

A pot either made of metal or earthenware used to cook broths and other food items is Marmite. Petite Marmite is a broth prepared in it.

89) What is Saucière/Sauce boat?

A hollowware used for serving sauces and gravies is Saucière. Few refer it as gravy boat too.

90) What is Chambong champagne glassware?

It's a 6 oz. glassware with a funnel stem attachment used to serve champagne.

91) What is Spork?

It's an equipment that is similar to spoon but with tines at the tip.

92) What is Splayd?

Splayd is an equipment that features the functions of spoon, fork and knife.

93) Name an Indian firm that manufactures edible spoons.

Bakey's, Hyderabad.

94) What is a Coaster?

Coaster made of wood, cardboard and plastic are used on tables wither under the glassware or bottles to save the table from water marks.

95) What is a Muddler?

Muddler is a bar equipment made of wood or stainless steel used for crushing fruits, herbs, sugar cubes and ice. The essential oils and juices will be released from fruits through this process called as muddling.

96) Name few measuring tools used in bar.

Jigger, peg measure, posi pour, measuring cups and spoons.

97) Differentiate Jigger from Peg measure.

Criteria of differentiation	Jigger	Peg measure
Measurement	Has got 2 cones with different measurements- 20 ml and 40 ml, 25 ml and 50 ml etc.	Has got 2 cones with different measurements-30 ml and 60 ml.
Extra attachment	Sometimes comes with an iron rod for easy pouring.	Comes without an iron rod.

98) Differentiate Cocktail shaker from Boston shaker

Criteria of differentiation	Cocktail shaker	Boston shaker
Parts	Has got 3 parts-Base, Strainer and Cap.	Has got 2 parts-A metallic tumbler and a fibre/glass tumbler.
Price	Cheaper in comparison to Boston Shaker.	Expensive in comparison to Cocktail Shaker.
Strainer	Uses in-built strainer.	Uses a Hawthorne/Julep strainer for straining the drink.

99) What is a Pastry fork?

A pastry fork is a three tined fork used for having pastries and desserts. The third tine of the fork is wider, enabling the user to cut the pastry.

100) Name the equipment required for serving Absinthe.

Reservoir glassware and Absinthe spoon.

2.4 Food and Beverage Outlets

1) What is a Restaurant?

Restaurant is a commercial establishment that offers different cuisines and provides table and chairs for the customers who come to dine.

2) Give the origin of the term 'Restaurant'.

The word 'Restaurant' has been derived from the French word 'restaurer' which means 'to restore'.

3) What are the different terms used for 'restaurant' in different countries?

'Restaurante' in Spain, 'Ristorante' in Italy, 'Restaurang' in Sweden, 'Restoran' in Russia, 'Restauracia' in Poland and 'Bojanalay' in India.

4) What are Chain restaurants?

Chain restaurants are restaurants that are a part of a multi unit organization. They often share the same menu, purchase supplies and equipment co-operatively and follow operating procedures that have been standardized for every restaurant in the chain.

5) Give few examples for Chain restaurants.

Answer- Pizza Hut, KFC (Kentucky Fried Chicken), Wimpy etc.

6) What are Family style restaurants?

Family style restaurants are restaurants that have a fixed menu and fixed price, usually with diners seated at a communal table such as on bench seats.

7) What is a Speciality Restaurant?

Speciality restaurant is a type of restaurant that focuses mainly on one cuisine.

8) What is a Multi-cuisine restaurant?

The restaurant that promotes two or more cuisines for the customers is termed as Multi-cuisine restaurant.

9) What is the objective of ethnic restaurant?

Ethnic restaurant serves ethnic food to its clients.

10) What are Barbecue restaurants/Poolside Barbecue?

These restaurants are often located next to the swimming pool and provide food for the guests who wish to have barbecued food (made on charcoal grill).It's mostly an open air restaurant that functions only in the evenings.

11) What are Fine dining restaurants?

These are restaurants with high standards. The food is fairly expensive and offers patrons the finest in service and atmosphere

12) What is Coffee shop?

Coffee shop is a food and beverage outlet that is opened for 24 hours a day. This outlet is often located next to the lobby of the hotel. Food items are pre-plated and the service is less elaborate.

13) What are BYO/BYOB restaurants?

Bring Your Own Booze restaurants permit its guests to bring personal alcoholic beverage bottles (for consumption) to their outlets.

14) What is QSR/Quick Service Restaurant?

Quick Service Restaurants are those restaurants which focus on both fast food and quality service.

15) What is Bar/Permit Room?

A licensed F&B outlet that sells alcoholic beverages is termed as Bar. Non-alcoholic beverages and snacks are also provided.

16) What is Pub/Public Utility Bar?

The term 'pub' is a short form for Public Houses that are still common in England. This outlet serves both alcoholic and non-alcoholic beverages but special emphasis is on the service of draught beer.

17) What is Café/Coffee bar?

Café/Coffee bar is an outlet that serves different types of coffee (espresso, mocha) along with pastries, sandwiches etc.

18) Give three examples for Café chain units.

Barista, Café Coffee Day and Tata Starbucks.

19) What is Bistro?

Bistro is a type of small restaurant which is inexpensive. Food and alcohol are sold in a moderate price in an informal and relaxed environment.

20) What is Brasserie?

It's a French style restaurant or coffee shop that serves mainly beer, cider and other drinks along with seafood items.

21) What are Take away restaurants?

Take away restaurants or Grab-n-go restaurants have gained much popularity during the Covid times. These restaurants parcel meal or food items for the customers according to the order placed. The customer collects it from the counter after paying the bill and consumes the food elsewhere.

22) What are Drive-in restaurants?

It's a facility extended by restaurants in which the customer can sit in their personal vehicle, consume food and beverages served to them according to the order placed.

23) What are Drive-thru restaurants?

A type of F&B outlet located at highways or near petrol pumps and has only a path around the outlet for vehicles to enter and exit. It has one or two counters where the attendant takes the order, collects payment and at the other counter guest collects the food. Food is not consumed in the premises.

24) What is Room Service?

Serving food and beverages in guest rooms of hotels is termed as Room Service. This service is available only for the resident guests.

25) What are the different types of Room Service?

Centralised Room Service and De-centralised Room Service.

26) What is a Pastry/Cake shop?

A pastry or a cake shop is often attached to a hotel for the sales of bakery products and beverages.

27) What is Cafeteria?

Cafeteria is an area allotted for the consumption of food and non-alcoholic beverages. The customers form line, collect their own food from a counter or table and take it to an eating area. The food is often grouped together, with hot foods kept in hot service containers (e.g. - bain-marie or hot plates), cold food in refrigerated cabinets and some food in the display cabinets.

28) What are fast food outlets?

Fast food outlets are those F&B outlets that primarily serve quick snacks and finger food items. They emphasize on 'speedy service'.

29) Give examples for International fast food chain outlets.

McDonald's, Subway, Pizza Hut, Burger King etc.

30) What is a Steak/Chop house?

Steak houses feature the preparation and service of beef steaks along with finger chips, baked potatoes and glazed vegetables as its accompaniments.

31) What are Food courts?

Food court includes few numbers of individual counters from where customers may either order and eat, or buy from a number of counters and eat in separate area.

32) What are Food Kiosks/Booths?

Food Kiosks are units that provide food to clients in areas such as parks, picnic spots, stadium theatres etc.

33) What are Themed restaurants?

Themed restaurants will have a particular theme. The entire concept of the restaurant revolves around the theme.

34) What is a brewpub?

Brewpub is a type of F&B outlet that works by combining both its restaurant and brewery. It sells most of the beer in the restaurant itself.

35) What is discotheque?

Guests dance to recorded music (sometimes live band too) and enjoy drinks in discotheques. Food is served mainly in the form of snacks and alcoholic beverages are served. Some discotheques follow dress codes and entry is restricted to its members only.

2.5 Food and Beverage Staff

1) Who is F&B Manager?

He/She is the head of Food and Beverage Service department of the hotel. He/She is responsible for the smooth running of different F&B outlets functioning in the hotel.

2) Who is Restaurant Manager?

Restaurant Manager is the departmental head of the restaurant. He is solely responsible for the proper running of the restaurant, lounge and grill room (includes maintaining high standards of food, service, health and safety)

3) Who is Maître d'hôtel?

Maître d'hôtel is the French name for Senior Captain of a restaurant. He has the overall responsibility of the restaurant and oversees the mise en place and mise en scene. He prepares the duty charts and also takes the order from the guests.

4) Who is a Sommelier?

Sommelier is a French term used to denote wine waiter. A sommelier should posses thorough knowledge of wines and its serving methods. He is responsible for taking the wine orders from the clients and deals with its service. A good sommelier is an efficient sales person and is knowledgeable about wines and the dishes it accompany.

5) Who is an Aboyeur/Barker/Announcer?

Aboyeur is a F&B staff often seen in the hot plate section of kitchen. He controls the hot plate section and is responsible for the effective communication between kitchen and the service team.

6) Who is a Trancheur?

A Trancheur, also known as carver is responsible for carving and portioning meat upon guest's request in a restaurant. He carves in a carving trolley and plates up each slice of meat in the most attractive manner. A good trancheur possess carving skills and will be aware of the joints of meat. He is also responsible for the making of accompaniments that tag along with the meat.

7) Who is Commis de rang?

French term for waiter. He is responsible for serving food and beverages to the guests.

8) Who is Debarrasseur/Bus boy?

Debarrasseur is a French term and Bus boy is an American term for Clearer. He uses a bussing trolley or bus box to clear the used operating equipments from the guests' table.

9) Who is a Runner?

Runner is an American term used for the member of a food and beverage service team who shuttles between the kitchen and the banquet floor carrying food items.

10) Who is le chef d'etage/Floor waiter?

The floor waiter takes care of the service of food and beverages in different floors of the hotel. In small hotels, the service might be limited to EMT and breakfast. The guest is served in the room by the floor waiters according to the guest's order and they posses good knowledge of both food and beverages.

11) Who is Le garçon de salle/Lounge waiter?

He takes care mainly of the beverage service in lounges and other public areas of the hotel. Alcoholic and non-alcoholic beverages, morning and afternoon tea are offered according to the guest's request. These waiters work on rotation basis and are also responsible for the cleanliness of the lounge area.

12) Who is Chef de wagon/Trolley waiter?

He is generally seen standing next to different trolleys such as salad trolley, dessert trolley, cheese trolley etc. responsible for carrying out service from different trolleys. He should assist the guest while selecting the food items from the trolley and must have good knowledge about the dishes displayed on the trolley.

13) Who is a Bar back?

Bar back is a term used to denote a trainee working in a bar. He assists the bartender to provide efficient service.

14) Who is chef de buffet?

He stands next to the buffet and controls the replenishing of the food items. A member of the kitchen brigade performs the role of Chef de buffet during the restaurant hours of operation.

15) Who is a Restaurateur?

A Restaurateur is a person who owns and manages a restaurant.

16) Who is a Back Waiter?

A back waiter assists front waiters in carrying out the work in the best possible manner. He clears used plate and replenishes table supplies.

17) Who is a Cicerone?

Cicerone is a beer professional who specializes in the service of different styles of beer and has sound knowledge about beer.

18) Mention any four personal attributes of F&B staff.

Short hair, no beard, trimmed moustache and well ironed uniform.

19) Give any four professional attributes of F&B staff.

Courteous behavior, punctuality, suggestive selling and knowledge of food and beverages.

20) Give the English, French and American terms used for different F&B staff.

English term	French term	American term
Banquet Manager	Directeur du banquet	-
Restaurant Manager	Directeur du restaurant	-
Reception head waiter	Maître d'hôtel de réception	-
Hostess	Hôtesse	-
Head waiter	Maître d'hôtel	Senior Captain
Carver	Le Trancheur	-

Wine waiter	Sommelier/Chef de vin	Wine butler
Station waiter	Chef de rang	Captain
Assistant station waiter	Demi chef de rang	Junior Captain
Waiter	Commis de rang/le serveur	Steward/Server
Waitress	La serveuse	Stewardess
Clearer	Débarasseur	Bus boy
Apprentice	Apprentis	Trainee
Floor waiter	Le chef d'étage	-
Lounge waiter	Le garçon de salle	-
Announcer	Aboyeur	Barker

2.6 Menu

1) Define menu.

Montagne (1981) defined a menu as a 'sheet of paper or cardboard on which is written, in a specific order, the names of all the dishes which are to be served in succession at a given meal'.

2) What is the meaning of the word 'menu'?

The French term 'menu' means 'in minute detail'. It also means 'bill of fare' or 'a detailed small list'.

3) What is the purpose of menu?

- ➢ To provide the information about the food and beverage along with its prices to the clients

- ➢ To make the customers aware of the sequence of the meal and courses

> ➢ To guide the guest in selecting his/her choice and placing the order

> ➢ To help the F&B production staff to prepare the food accordingly and to enable the

> ➢ F&B Service staff to do the cover set up and to serve promptly.

4) Who used to refer a sheet of paper while having food in order to reserve his appetite for his favourite dishes?

Duke Henry of Brunswick.

5) What are the different types of menu?

A la carte menu, Table d'hôte menu, Function menu, Cyclic menu, Carte du jour, Plat du jour etc.

6) What is A la carte menu?

Literally means 'from the card'. The dishes that are listed in an a la carte menu card are priced individually and the portion size of the dish served is considerably more. The customer is free to choose any food or beverage item from an a la carte menu card. Most of the dining establishments that offer a la carte menu might feature all the 17 courses with a good number of choices.

7) Give few advantages of A la carte menu.

> ➢ Vast choices of food and beverages

> ➢ Allows consumers to eat light or heavy

> ➢ Hotel can gain more profit through regional specialities.

8) Give few disadvantages of A la carte menu.

> ➢ Takes more time for preparation

> ➢ Service professionals required for the service

> ➢ Some food items might not sell as they are highly priced.

9) What is Table d'hôte menu?

Literally means 'table of the host' and is mostly known as TDH/Fixed menu/Prix Fixe. It's a fixed price menu with limited choices. The set price is charged whether or not the entire meal is consumed. Most of the dining establishments that offer table d'hôte menu might feature a three course menu which includes appetizer, main course and dessert along with coffee.

10) Give few advantages of Table d'hôte menu.

> ➢ Cost control is possible

> ➢ Little food wastage

> ➢ Price charges are relatively simple.

11) Give few disadvantages of Table d'hôte menu.

> ➢ Guest may feel the food costs too much

> ➢ Choices are limited

> ➢ Guest might still feel hungry as the portion size is controlled.

12) Differentiate A la carte menu from Table d'hôte menu

Criteria of differentiation	A la carte menu	Table d'hôte menu
Meaning	'From the card.'	'Table of the host.'
Pricing	Food and beverage items are individually priced.	Food and beverage items are collectively priced.
Preparation time	Takes more time for food preparation.	Takes less time for food preparation.
Portion size	Large.	Comparatively smaller to a la carte.
Cover setting	Done after the guest places the order.	Done before the guest's arrival.

13) What is Function menu?

Also known as Banquet menu and is often offered during wedding receptions, birthday or anniversary celebrations. The host often selects a table d'hôte menu for fixed price and the number of courses depends on the nature of the function.

14) What is Cyclic menu?

Cyclic menu is a series of fixed meals which are rotated over time. This menu is mostly followed in hostels and hospitals. It has limited choice for three meals in the day and can be planned to give a balanced diet. A cycle can be from 5 days to 5 or more weeks.

15) What is Carte du jour?

This term means 'card of the day' or 'feature of the day'. It's often used in F&B outlets as an adjunct to the regular menu. Carte du jour can be offered daily, weekly or on cyclical basis. The food items mentioned is supposed to be totally different from those included in the regular menu. This card should not be made to get rid of leftovers.

16) What is Plat du jour?

Literally means 'dish of the day'. When a dish is in the plat du jour it's on the a la carte menu at a fixed price, often less than the price normally charged for it on other days. This is frequently a main dish of the table d'hôte menu.

17) What is Kid's/Children's menu?

Kid's menu is a type of menu created according to the taste of kids. It might feature doughnuts, french fries, mini pizzas, burgers and sandwiches, cheese fingers etc. The menu will be colourful, includes puzzles and cartoon characters.

18) What is Take away menu?

Take away menu is seen in restaurants that has the take away option. It's a small booklet menu that features food and beverage items that could be prepared in the restaurant and eaten elsewhere.

19) What is Digital menu?

Digital menu displays the names of dishes and its rates digitally.

20) What is QR code menu?

A menu which one can view after scanning the QR code given, using the mobile device. It's relevance was felt more during the Covid-19 as the focus shifted to contactless services.

21) What is Online menu?

A menu which is available online and can be accessed by the customers with the help of internet is termed as an online menu.

22) What is Diet menu?

A menu designed according to the dietary requirements of the customer is a Diet menu.

23) What is a Beverage list?

A Beverage list includes both alcoholic and non-alcoholic beverages but particularly soft drinks, mocktails, cocktails, wines, beer, spirits, coffee, tea etc. The number of pages of a beverage list tends to be more than a normal wine list since it covers a wide range of beverages.

24) What is a Wine list?

A wine list exhibits all the wines that are available for sales in the outlet. The sommelier should be able to advise and suggest wines from the wine list to the guests.

25) What is Static Menu?

A menu that remains unchanged for a period of one year is termed as a Static menu.

26) What is Degustation/Tasting menu?

A menu offered to the customers for the purpose of tasting and providing their feedback about the dishes.

27) What is a door knob menu card?

A menu card meant for the resident guests of a hotel which is hung on the guest door's knob at around midnight.

28) What are the different menus based on the meal periods?

Breakfast menu, Brunch menu, Luncheon menu, Afternoon tea menu, High tea menu, Supper menu etc.

29) What is Cigar menu?

A Cigar menu is offered in a cigar bar and it features variety of cigars available for sales.

30) What is Ice cream menu?

An ice cream menu will have various varieties of ice creams such as cassata, bombe, banana split etc. to choose from.

2.7 Food and Beverage Service Terminology

ABC of a cover-Ashtray, Budvase and Cruet set.

Alcoholic beverage-Beverage with 5% or more of ethyl alcohol.

Asparagus Tongs-Asparagus tongs is a special service equipment used to hold asparagus in tact.

Au-A French term that has the same meaning as 'a la' meaning 'in the manner of', 'in the style of' and 'according to'. In cooking, this phrase designates the style of preparation or a particular garnish.

- **au beurre-**Made with or in butter.

- **au bleu-**Means blue and describes the process where freshly killed fish is plunged into boiling water and poached until the skin of the fish has a bluish tinge.

- **au fromage-**The term means cheese and means made with or in cheese.

- **au gratin-**To dress up vegetables, meats, and fish with a layer of bread crumbs and/or grated cheese on top. It is then broiled or baked until a thin brown crust forms.

- **au jus-**Describes meat served in its own natural juices, not with gravy.

- **au naturel-**Means natural or simple. It refers to foods which are served very simply or which are uncooked.

- **au poivre-**Means pepper and means cooked with pepper.

Au lait-The term means 'with milk'.

Bread boat/basket-A basket primarily designed to keep the bread items on a table.

Briefing-Briefing is done prior to the opening of the banquets/restaurant. It's the meeting of the banquet/restaurant brigade (staff) with the outlet manager. In this session, the senior most staff gives the instructions (non-availabilities of the restaurant, restaurant table reservations, table allocations of the staff etc) and checks certain aspects of service (Grooming of the staff, Things in waiter's kit etc.).

Beurre-French word for 'butter'.

- **beurre manie-**French term for a kneaded mixture of butter and flour.

- **beurre noir-**French for sweet butter that has been cooked until it has just turned a light shade of brown. Wine vinegar, capers, and parsley are then added.

Bus box-Bus box either made of plastic or metal is a box used by the bus boy to clear a dirty table.

Bussing-A restaurant term used for clearing off and resetting tables after guests have left. In busier restaurants this is done by the busboy (busser) using a bus box/bussing trolley.

Campers-A term used to denote guests who finished their meals but still occupies the table. They can obstruct the restaurant business by limiting the seating capacity.

Canapé-Small piece of bread, either plain or toasted and topped with meats, vegetables and fruits

Central appointments of a cover (6 essentials of a cover)-Ashtray, Budvase, Cruet set, Table number, Menu card holder and Butter dish.

Commis-An assistant in the restaurant brigade.

Cover-The space taken by the guest to consume his/her meal is termed as a Cover. It is the space allotted on the table for the cutlery, crockery and glassware for one person. Ashtray, Budvase, Cruet set and Table number are also included in a Cover. The size of a cover is 24 inches × 18 inches.

Cruet set-Cruet set is a set of salt cellar, pepper caster and mustard pot.

Crumbing/Brushing down-This term is used when the waiter crumbs the table i.e., collects the debris from the table. A B&B plate, knife and a clean napkin is used by the waiter for this purpose.

Dash-A traditional measure of volume, refers to a small amount of a seasoning that is added to a dish by a quick downward stroke of the hand and is approximately 1/16 or 1/8 of a teaspoon.

De-briefing-De-briefing is done after a function gets over/the restaurant is closed. It's the closing meeting of the banquet/restaurant brigade (staff) with the Banquet/Restaurant Manager. Feedback of the guests is given to the staff during this session.

Doily paper-A small, round ornamental paper used in saucers and B&B plates to safe guard them from stains.

Dumb waiter-A small elevator often seen in large hotels and mansions used to transport food from one floor to the other.

Dummy waiter-Dummy waiter is a type of furniture used in the restaurant for keeping all the service equipments. It is used as a landing table for the dishes picked up from the kitchen enroute to the table. Dummy waiter is taken care by the waiter and trainees. They equip this furniture with salvers, finger bowls, KOT books, water jugs, plates and different kinds of table ware. Dummy waiter is also known as Side board/Service console or side station.

Eight-Six (86)-If the kitchen runs out of a particular dish, the dish is termed as '86'.

Ergonomics-An applied science that involves studying the characteristics of people and designing or arranging their activities so that they are done in a safer and efficient manner. For example planning easy entrance to and exit from the facility.

Espresso-The term 'Espresso' means 'to press' or 'to press out' in Italian. The coffee beans are grinded into the powder form (very fine) and it is packed inside a small filter basket in the espresso machine. Hot water is then pressed through the powder and the result is a very strong aromatic coffee.

Espresso machine-A machine that prepares espresso coffee. The machine heats and holds hot water and pumps it under pressure through coffee in a sieve to make espresso.

Etiquette-Rules of correct behaviour.

Eyes-These are holes found in some cheeses. It's formed by gases released during aging.

Gratuities-Money given to the server by the guest for his services rendered. Also known as Tips.

In the Weeds-A restaurant slang/term that means it is really, really busy. For example, if the kitchen has several orders placed and they are having a hard time in the kitchen then, they are "in the weeds."A waiter who has too many clients to be served at once is yet an other example.

Inventory-The term inventory refers to the total number of goods and materials stored in a department at any given point of time. The departmental manager or the store keeper is held responsible for the stock taking of the materials on a regular basis in order to prepare the purchase list. Most of the items are kept at par.

Lounge service-This service is often seen in 5 star hotels. Generally hotels with lounge service might not feature a coffee shop. Morning coffee, afternoon tea and even service of alcoholic beverages are carried out as a part of lounge service. The staff who carries out the lounge service works on shift basis.

Magic phrases-These are the phrases used either by the host or hostess to welcome or part with the guest.

Mise en place-This term is widely used in day-to-day hotel operations especially in F&B department. Mise-en-place is a French term that means 'put in place'. By this term one mean to arrange and assemble service equipments before the guests actually arrive in a restaurant. Normally this task is given to the F&B service apprentice and this job is monitored by a waiter. Cleaning and filling water jugs, cruet set, sugar dredger is an example for Mise en place.

Mise en scene-It means 'prepare the environment of the outlet' before service. Preparing the restaurant as a welcome area for the guests who are coming to dine is what mise en place is all about. It includes creating ambience with regard to cleanliness, music, proper state of furniture, controlling the temperature etc.

Nip-An Australian standard measure of 30 ml.

Nouvelle cuisine-It's a type of cuisine that involves a distinctive style and presentation with a lighter and more innovative approach. The emphasis is put on more natural presentation of food.

Paper parasol-A fancy decorative item used on cocktails and mocktails just before service. It increases the eye appeal of the drink and the term implies a light weight umbrella made from paper.

Par stock-It's the level of an inventory item that must be maintained at all times. In F&B service department it is the F&B manager who normally determines the par stock.

Placemats-Placemats are used on restaurant tables and bar counters. They are thick, protects the table and counter from heat and many are water-resistant so that spills will not seep through and stain the table.

POS System-A point of sale system is a computer system that helps businesses track sales. It also tracks employee sales (who sold the most during a shift) and which dishes are sold most often.

Posi-pour-A measure used in bar which is similar to optic measure. It's less bulky and measurer the quantity of spirit poured

Salt cellar-A small receptacle used for serving salt, normally placed on a table. Also known as Salière.

Stiffed-A restaurant term used to describe when a customer does not pay a gratuity for service in a situation where a gratuity is expected.

Sugar dredger-A container kept on table filled with either icing or caster sugar. In French, Glacière à sucre.

Swizzle stick- Used by the guests to mix the drink. It's either made of plastic or glass.

Tongs-Tongs are designed to hold or lift food items from the containers or pots. Tongs comes in different sizes and are normally made of stainless steel.

Urn-A closed steel container, usually with a spout used mainly for serving tea and coffee

Yorkshire pudding-A traditional accompaniment of Roast Beef and is made from a batter of flour, eggs and milk. Later, the batter is baked in an oven and served.

Zester-A bar equipment used to cut the zest from citrus fruit. It has a holder and a flat blade with five small holes.

CHAPTER-3

Buffets & Banquets

Section no.	Sub-heading	Questions
3.1	Buffets	25
3.2	Banquets	30
3.3	Meal Periods	30
3.4	Types of Service methods	20
3.5	Cigar, Cigarette & Pipe tobacco	70

3.1 Buffets

1) What is Buffet?

Buffet is display of food and beverages in a counter for guests. The cooked food is kept in chafing dishes and buffets are normally used in conjunction with a restaurant or banquet.

2) What type of service is seen in buffets?

Self service or assisted service.

3) How restaurant buffet is different from buffet in banquets?

In the case of a restaurant buffet, the guests pay a fixed price for the buffet and he or she can eat as much as they want from the buffet counter. The host of the banquet function makes the final payment once the function gets over. The guests are free to have whatever they want from the buffet counter.

4) Give few examples for buffet equipment.

Buffet table, Chafing dish, Ladle, Lazy Susan, Beverage fountains etc.

5) What is a Chafing dish?

Chafing dish is an operating equipment used to keep the food warm in a buffet counter.

6) Name the parts of a chafing dish.

A Chafing dish consists of five parts-a metallic frame, fuel dish, water pan, food pan and a top.

7) What is a Lazy Susan?

Lazy Susan is generally a wooden, circular rotating tray that holds different types of food items which is placed on a buffet counter.

8) What are the different types of buffets?

Fork buffet, Finger buffet and Sit down buffet.

9) What is a fork buffet?

A buffet that involves food items which can be easily picked up with the help of a fork is termed as Fork buffet. The guest usually stands and holds the plate with one hand, consumes the food using a fork with the other hand. Guests tend to eat less as it is uneasy to eat without a table. Light buffet items are served like sausage and bacon rolls, sandwiches, bridge rolls, sweets and beverages.

10) What is finger buffet?

Finger buffet is a type of buffet that can be served at any time of a day when guests are not anticipating substantial amount of food. Flatware and cutleries are not used and the guest uses his finger to consume the food. Finger bowls and large napkins are provided for the guests.

11) What is sit down buffet?

This kind involves buffet spread with seating arrangements. It's a semi-formal style in which the guest selects the food items from the buffet counter, sits down at a set table. Sit down buffet is ideal for company meetings involving dinner, staff get-together, private parties, etc.

12) What is full buffet?

A full buffet is a main meal, which includes a wonderful array of food displays in the dining room. Tables and chairs are offered to the guests and the cover is laid well in advance.

13) What is normal buffet?

In a normal buffet, the guests collects their food, utensils, beverages etc. from the buffet counter and the service staff takes care of the cleaning part of the buffet tables.

14) What is a modified buffet?

A modified buffet makes the service staff to serve beverages and dessert courses while the guests obtain the appetizers, salads and main course by themselves from the buffet counter.

15) What is a deluxe buffet?

Deluxe buffet service includes more professionalism. The banquet staff serves almost all the courses to the guests except the main course.

16) What is high tea buffet?

A buffet set for high tea is termed as high tea buffet. The buffet counter will feature varieties of sandwiches, baked goods, pastries, desserts and tea.

17) What is a display buffet?

Different types of display items like ice carvings, vegetable and fruit carvings, butter sculptures, flambé items, live food preparations etc. are seen in a display buffet.

18) What is a theme buffet?

A theme buffet is a particular buffet that focuses on a theme. The items and displays laid on the counter will be related to the theme.

19) What is Smorgasbord/ Smörgåsbord?

A Scandinavian buffet that features a wide array of dishes which includes hors'doeuvre items, smoked and pickled fish, sandwiches, salads, cheeses, hot and cold meat items, relishes etc is Smorgasbord. Aquavit, Brännvin, Beer and Coffee are also served.

20) What is Seafood/Oyster buffet?

Oyster buffet serves different types of seafood items but primarily oysters. The accompaniments for the sea food items such as sauces and condiments are also placed in the buffet.

21) What is Meal period buffet?

A buffet which is arranged according to various meal periods of a particular day is meal period buffet. Examples include Breakfast buffet, Brunch buffet, Lunch buffet, Afternoon tea buffet etc.

22) Give some principles that one has to bear in his/her mind while setting up buffets.

- ➢ Buffet should look eye appealing, neat and appetizing

- ➢ All hot food items should be served hot and all cold food items cold

- ➢ Avoid rush in the buffet counter

- ➢ Sufficient service staff should be available in the buffet counter

- ➢ A printed or typed menu card placed on the dining table or a poster sized menu near to the buffet table provides information about the various food items that are displayed and it adds to the enjoyment of the guest.

23) How buffets influence the meal experience?

The overall appearance of a buffet counter can stimulate the appetite of the diner because of its charm, magnetism, excitement, flavor and aroma. The attractively presented buffet table his/her mind will subconsciously generate interest in their minds.

24) Give any two advantages of buffet.

- ➢ Variety of food items could be displayed for the guests.

- ➢ Less no. of staff required for food service.

25) Mention any two disadvantages of buffet.

- ➤ No personalized service for customers.

- ➤ Food wastage.

3.2 Banquets

1) What is Banquet?

Banquet means sumptuous feast given to large crowd of guests. Banquet is a meal experience that has a menu pre determined by the host for all the guests attending that particular event.

2) Name few functions that are conducted in banquet halls

Wedding receptions, birthday and anniversary celebrations, conferences, seminars, product launches etc.

3) From which word is the term 'banquet' derived?

The term is derived from the French word 'Banc' which means benches.

4) Which is the highest revenue generating outlet in the F&B Service department?

Banquets.

5) Who is the head of Banquet department?

Banquet manager.

6) Which are the different types of banquets?

Formal, Informal and Semi-formal.

7) What is Formal banquet?

Formal banquet is a banquet that is of serious nature. The dignitaries are seated at the head table and the remaining guests are seated facing the head table. The banquet staff serves to the guests on the table and will also do the clearance according to the instructions of the banquet captain. The order of service at the head table is very formal. Examples include birthday parties of kings and queens of the Royal family, President of the other country's company visiting other country etc. During formal functions, the guest of honour and the host is served exactly at the same time.

8) What are Semi-formal banquets?

Semi-formal banquets take place during company board meetings. These types of banquets are a combination of formal and informal banquets. The dignitaries or senior most managers are seated at the head table according to their ranks. The remaining crowd can occupy any individual table.

9) What are Informal banquets?

Informal banquets do not have any set plan for the seating arrangements. There is no head table and the guests can either stand or sit for having the meal.

10) What are State banquets?

These are banquets conducted in honour of high level dignitaries (VVIPs and VIPs).State banquets helps in establishing a good relationship between people. The food and beverage service staff who participates in a state banquet function are highly experienced professionals. They use high quality, polished operating equipments for the food service. The function is held in a larger banquet hall and the set up is table d'hôte. A head table is set for the chief guest and the remaining table arrangements might vary from round tables to square tables.

11) What is Banquet Function Diary/Book?

This book has the details of all the banquet bookings. Once the host has booked a banquet function the information pertaining to it will be entered here. The name of the host, name of the banquet hall, number of pax, date and time of the function and the rate of meal is noted down. The main purpose of the book is to avoid confusions and overbooking. Whenever a banquet booking comes, the banquet manager or the sales assistant refer the function diary to check whether the hall is available on that particular day requested by the host. Today, this book has been replaced with the use of computer softwares.

12) What is Banquet Function Prospectus (BFP or FP)?

FP or Function Prospectus is a banquet document prepared by the Banquet department. It is through this form that the details of the forthcoming banquet function is informed to other departments like F&B Production, House Keeping, Front Office, Security etc.

13) What are the different types of bars seen in banquets?

Open, Cash bars and Portable bars.

14) What is an Open bar?

The guest can come to this banquet bar counter during the function and consume the alcoholic beverage the host has ordered. The guest need not pay anything. The host can be charged for open bar in different ways. The first way is that the host is charged only for the liquor bottles that are opened. The second way is that the host is charged only for the amount of liquor that is consumed by the guests. In some banquets, the guests are provided tickets/coupons for alcoholic beverages.

15) What are Cash bars?

In Cash bars, the guest who is consuming alcohol from the banquet bar counter has to pay for his drink. The host requests the banquet manager for a bar counter in the banquet hall. As cash bars bring less revenue to the hotel, the guest has to meet a minimum amount of liquor sales. Otherwise the host has to pay the work charges of the bartender.

16) What are Portable bars?

Portable bars are bars that can be easily set up and dismantled for the provision of drinks in banquets. An added advantage of this bar is that on short notice anywhere on the premises or outdoors alcoholic beverages can be served. A typical portable bar ranges in length from 4 -8 feet.

17) What is Corkage?

Corkage refers to charges made by a licensed establishment for providing service equipments like bottle openers, soda etc. to guests who bring their own alcoholic beverage for consumption in the hotel.

18) Who is a Banquet Sales Assistant?

A Banquet Sales Assistant takes care of the banquet bookings. He prepares the Banquet Function Prospectus (BFP) with the details of the guest requirements and circulates it to the major departments of the hotel.

19) What are Sprigs?

A Sprig is a row of tables provided for the clients to consume meal.

20) What is Gangway?

Gangway is the space between two sprigs. The waiters use gangway to move and serve food to the clients.

21) What is an aisle?

Aisle is a walking space provided for the guests in a banquet hall.

22) What is Toasting?

Toasting is the act of raising the wine glasses in order to honour someone or something. Toasting is done by a toast master or the host during wedding receptions, engagement parties, retirement parties, celebrations of successful business etc.

23) Who is a Toast master?

A Toast Master is a person who raises or announces the toast in a formal function. He is also known as Master of Ceremony (MC/emcee) of the function. A Toast Master should possess good communication skills and should have presence of mind.

24) What are the common types of banquet arrangements/set ups/seating arrangements?

'U' shape arrangement, Theatre style arrangement, Classroom style arrangement, Board Room style arrangement, Box (Conference) shape arrangement, Fish Bone arrangement etc.

25) What are Air walls in banquets?

A moveable partition or panel with which a bigger banquet hall could be sub-divided into smaller areas.

26) What is 'cut-off' date in banquets?

It's the date by which the client must either book or release the banquet hall which was tentatively held for him/her by the hotel.

27) What is 'lectern' in banquets?

It's a stand used in banquet functions for keeping paper, books or notes by speakers.

28) Name few Audio Visual (AV) equipment used in banquets.

OHP, LCD, Screen, Dimmer switch, Amplifier, Mixer, Microphone etc.

29) What is BEO?

Banquet Event Order.

30) Mention beverage service in banquets.

A waiter or a team of waiters are arranged specially for the service of beverages. The type of service depends on the beverages that have to be served. Cocktails, Mocktails, Aperitifs, Table wines, Sparkling wines, Digestifs, Soft drinks, Coffee etc. are some of the beverages that are commonly served during banquets. The beverages for each course should always be served before that course.

3.3 Meal Periods

1) What is Meal?

The dictionary says meal is 'the quantity of food taken at one time.' The instance of eating, specifically one that takes place at a specific time and includes specific, prepared food can be called as Meal.

2) Give different meal periods along with its timings.

Meal period	Timing
Early Morning Tea	0430 hrs to 0600 hrs
Breakfast	Continental-0600 hrs-0900 hrs English-0530 hrs-0930 hrs American-0530 hrs-0930 hrs
Brunch	0900 hrs-1400 hrs
Elevenses	1100 hrs
Lunch	1200 hrs-1500 hrs
Afternoon Tea	1500 hrs-1700 hrs
High Tea	1700 hrs-1900 hrs
Dinner	1800 hrs-2230 hrs
Supper	2030 hrs-0230 hrs and 2400 hrs-0700 hrs

3) What is Breakfast/ Petit déjeuner?

Breakfast is the first meal of the day as well as the most important meal of the day. The term is used as the fast of the night is broken.

4) What are the different types of Breakfast?

The breakfasts commonly seen are namely Continental Breakfast, English breakfast and American breakfast.

5) What is Continental breakfast?

A light breakfast menu that includes juices, hot croissants, brioche or toast, butter, preserves (jam, marmalades etc.), pastries and coffee. This traditional menu has been replaced nowadays with a variety of other food items that include fruits, juices, assorted breads, doughnuts, ham, cheese, cereals, muffins etc.

6) What is Café complet?

It means coffee along with Continental breakfast.

7) What is Thé complet?

Tea along with Continental breakfast.

8) What is Café simple?

The term implies just coffee and nothing else.

9) What is Thé simple?

Only tea will be served.

10) What is the cover for Continental breakfast?

Side plate with side knife, napkin, central appointments-ashtray, budvase, table number, sugar pot with sugar tongs, breakfast cup or tea cup along with a saucer and teaspoon, underplates for the pots, slop basin and strainer for tea. Once the guest is seated then the waiter should place the following items on the table-Butter dish with butter and alternatives, Preserves on a preserve dish, Toast rack with bread or Bread basket with bread rolls, Teapot/Coffee pot/hot or cold milk/hot water jug and other items according to the wish of the guest.

11) What is English breakfast?

English breakfast is popularly known as Full Breakfast menu as it's quite substantial. A cooked main course is normally served but the current trend offers fresh and stewed fruits along with juices, fish, eggs, cold cuts of meat (bacon), decaffeinated coffee, mineral water, muesli, yoghurt, etc

12) What is the cover for English breakfast?

The cover set up for English breakfast is very similar to a Table-d'hôte set up with the exception of the soup spoon. The cover includes side plate with side knife, napkin, central appointments-ashtray, budvase, table number, salt cellar, pepper caster, sugar dredger, sugar pot with sugar tongs, fish knife and fish fork, joint knife and joint fork, dessert spoon and dessert fork, breakfast cup or tea cup along with a saucer, teaspoon and underplates for the pots.

13) What is American breakfast?

American Breakfast is a type of breakfast include eggs that are either fried or poached, pan cakes with syrups, cereals, bread toasts with preserves, hot beverage (tea or coffee) and fruit juices

14) What is Buffet breakfast?

Buffet breakfast is a very popular concept and involves food and beverage items being served in a buffet counter as part of a particular breakfast. Most of the hotels give free buffet breakfast as part of Continental meal plan.

15) What are Preserves?

Preserves are thick fruit spreads made out of different fruits by cooking them in sugar. It includes assorted jams and marmalades.

16) What is Marmalade?

Marmalade is a preserve that looks very similar to jam and is made from citrus fruits like lemon, orange etc. It's normally served during breakfast along with toasted bread. The peel of the citrus fruit enhances the flavour.

17) What is Indian Breakfast?

Indian breakfast often called as 'Nastha' varies widely between south and north. It's simple and mainly vegetarian items are served. Hotels provide Indian breakfast between 0600-1000 hrs.

18) What is North Indian breakfast?

A type of breakfast that includes several Indian breads like Naan, Paratha, Aloo Paratha, Kulcha etc. topped with a hot beverage i.e., milk, coffee or tea. Spicy vegetables and dal are the accompaniments along with few Indian sweets. Yogurt and sweet lassi might also be served. Breakfast also varies from region to region.

19) What is South Indian breakfast?

South Indian breakfast consists of different variations of idly and dosas with chutney and sambhar as the accompaniments. Vada, Upma, Chapathi, Pongal, Puttu, Appam etc. are commonly the specialties of South Indian breakfast. Bread toast, jam, butter, omelets too are preferred by people. Coffee, tea, bournvitta, badam with milk etc. are the most common beverages.

20) What is Brunch/Bruncheon?

Brunch is a meal period that combines both breakfast and lunch. It is seen mainly on Sundays and holidays, often happens after a morning event or proceeding to an afternoon one. Fruit juices, cereals, breads and preserves are offered to the guest. Apart from these substantial items like meats, eggs, vegetables, fruits and cheeses are served. This American concept is believed to have been derived from the European late breakfast and Chinese Yum Cha.

21) What is Elevenses/Goŭter?

This meal (very common in United Kingdom) includes snack items like biscuits, cake and a cup of tea and is often offered to children. An elevenses is similar to afternoon tea but the latter is taken during noon. The items served are less savoury than brunch.

22) What is Luncheon/Lunch/Déjeuner?

The food items differ according to the guest preferences. Both a la carte and table d'hôte menus are used during lunch period. The table d'hôte menus offered during lunch time features less number of courses as the guest might be too busy with his work. Even the items are served more quickly than the dinner meal. Hotel offers different cuisines at reasonable prices. Some hotels provides buffet counter for a fixed price and this practice is quite common these days. Indian lunch include Vegetarian thali and Non-vegetarian thali, different varieties of biriyanis, pulao, Indian breads with dal. Hors'doeuvres, soups, pasta/rice items, stews, meat roasts, grilled meats, vegetable and potatoes, cold meat items, cheeses, soufflés, puddings, cakes, fresh fruits, coffee etc. can also be served. The cover set up depends on the meal order.

23) What is Afternoon Tea?

Baked food items like breads with preserves, pastries, cakes etc., assorted sandwiches, scones hot beverages like tea and coffee are served between. In some restaurants, food is often served on a tiered stand. The cover for afternoon tea includes side plate with side knife, napkin, central appointments-ashtray, budvase, table number, sugar pot with sugar tongs, pastry fork, tea cup along with a saucer and teaspoon, tea pot, jug of cold/hot milk, hot water jug (optional), butter dish with butter knife, preserve with a saucer and preserve spoon, slop basin with a tea strainer and underplates for the pots. Items like beverages both hot and cold, butter dish, preserve dish etc. are placed in front of the guest once he/she is seated. Extra flatware and cutleries can also be placed according to the guest's order. The range of teas on offer can vary from half a dozen to over a hundred, including some very rare and obscure ones. Examples are Cream tea, Assam tea, Darjeeling tea etc.

24) What is Cream tea?

When the guest has ordered for cream tea, scones (fruit or plain), may be served warm along with either clotted or whipped cream. Strawberry jam is offered but butter is served only upon request.

25) What is Champagne cream tea?

Champagne cream tea is cream tea served along with a glass of champagne.

26) What is High tea/Meat tea?

High Tea is a variation of Afternoon Tea and is considered as a substitute for both afternoon tea and the evening meal. Apart from the items served for afternoon tea it offers cold meat items, grilled meat dishes, salads, fish, egg and hence it's popularly known as 'Meat Tea'. The cover for high tea includes side plate with side knife, napkin, central appointments-ashtray, budvase, table number, salt and pepper, mustard and mustard spoon, sugar pot with sugar tongs, joint knife and joint fork, tea cup along with a saucer and teaspoon, tea pot, jug of cold/hot milk, hot water jug (optional), butter dish with butter knife, preserves with a saucer and preserve spoon, slop basin with a tea strainer, underplate for the pots. Items like beverages both hot and cold, butter dish, preserve dish etc. are placed in front of the guest once he/she is seated. Extra flatware and cutleries can also be placed according to the guest's order.

27) Name few accompaniments offered to the guests during High tea.

HP sauce, mustard sauce, tomato ketchup and Worcestershire sauce.

28) What is Dinner/Diňer?

The term Diňer is derived from the Latin disjunare. Some people consider dinner as the last meal of the day. Guest often relax and want to enjoy a real meal experience during this meal period. Compared to lunch, a good number of courses are planned and offered to the clients. It might begin with an aperitifs list and end with a sweet wine. A simple dinner menu comprises of a meat, fish, poultry, vegetables and/or with bread or rice. Dinner is more formal in comparison to supper. A dinner menu might feature hors'doeuvres, soups, pasta/rice items, sorbets, stews, meat roasts, grilled meats, salads, vegetable and potatoes, cold meat items, savoury items, cheeses, soufflés, puddings, cakes, fresh fruits, coffee etc.

29) What is Supper/Souper?

This meal is not that common in India but is a less formal evening meal consumed after watching a theatre show or a movie. The concept is very popular in Europe and the dishes served are less substantial. A typical supper menu might include three courses that vary from hors'doeuvres and soups (limited) to fish or grilled meats with vegetables and potatoes or cold buffet with salad and sweets, desserts and coffee.

30) What is an Express breakfast?

Food and beverage items served to the guests in the guest room according to their time of convenience are termed as Express breakfast. Many hotels follow the concept of door knob menu card for fulfilling the same purpose.

3.4 Types of Service Methods

1) What are the factors that determine the style of service in any F&B outlet?

Type of establishment, menu type, location of the outlet, time available for the meal, targeted customers, turnover expected and cost of the meal served.

2) Classify Food and beverage service methods.

Table service, Assisted service, Self service, Single point service and In situ/Specialized service.

3) What are the different forms of Table service?

French service, English service, Russian service, American service and Gueridon service.

4) What is French service?

The food is brought in platters by the waiter. The platter is placed on the table and the waiter retreats. The food is portioned and divided by the guests themselves according to their preference. The waiter removes or replenishes the platter. In this type of service more emphasis is given on food presentation.

5) What is English service?

English service is also known as 'Silver Service' and 'Platter to plate service'. After the order is taken, the plates are placed on the table by the waiter from the right hand side of the guest. Then the food is brought on platters and is offered to the host for approval. Once he/she approves the food, the waiter serves the food to the guests from the left hand side. After serving everyone the platters are either left on the side station or in a hot cupboard. This service originated in England and is a type of service where most of the work is done by the server, except the approval of food which is done by the host.

6) What is Russian service?

Russian service is a combination of the French and English forms of service. The food on the platters is taken to the side board, where portioning and garnishing is done in the full view of guests. Later, the platter is handed over to the guests who help themselves and the food replenishment is done by the waiter at the side board.

7) What is American service?

American service is also known as 'Pre-plated service' and is the simplest form of service. The food is brought pre-plated (placed on plate) from the kitchen itself. The food is individually portioned, plated and garnished in the kitchen, and placed on the table from the right hand side of the guest. This kind of service is widely used in coffee shops and in other fast food outlets. Plating food requires care and good supervision.

8) What is Gueridon service?

Gueridon service is done using a special type of trolley called Gueridon trolley. A gueridon trolley is a moveable trolley with rechaud or a gas stove and is equipped with chopping boards, knives, pans, different sauce bottles etc. The trolley is placed next to the guest's table where the food preparation are done. The food might be partially prepared in the kitchen and completed by the gueridon expert or headwaiter in full view of the client who had placed the order. The waiter carries out flambéing, filleting, carving, garnishing and portioning on the trolley. Some items that are served from Gueridon trolley include Anguille Fumée, Crepes Suzette, Pepper Steak, Banane Flambé etc.

9) What is Assisted service?

In this type of service, the waiter assists the guests in serving. It's mostly a combination of table and self service. Carvery service and Buffet service are good examples for assisted service.

10) What is Self service?

The client himself takes care of the service. He/she collects a tray and passes through different counters and picks his/her food. Self service is mostly seen in counter, free flow, echelon and supermarket.

11) What is Counter/Cafeteria service?

The customers form line, collect their own food from a counter or table and take it to an eating area. The food is often grouped together, with hot foods kept in hot service containers (e.g. - bain-marie or hot plates), cold food in refrigerated cabinets and some food in the display cabinets. In the staff cafeteria, after the meal, the staffs themselves clear the table and place the cutleries, flatware and crockery at a designated point where the washing up staff can collect it.

12) What is Buffet service?

This service includes a counter or table in which the food is displayed. The client helps themselves to as many of the items and as much food as they want. In some forms of buffet the waiter stands behind the counter and serve the clients. The portion size of the food is controlled by the waiters according to the instructions given by the Chef.

13) What is Carousel service?

This style of service consists of a circular counter that revolves slowly to display the meal items on offer. It is usually located in a wall or counter between the kitchen and the dining area. As the carousel passes through the kitchen the food items are replenished. The clients stand by the counter on the dining side, select items from the carousel as it revolves slowly and passes them.

14) What is Single point service?

In this type of service, the service to customers is from a single point. The meal purchased can be consumed on premises or taken away. This include Take away, Drive thru, Vending operations, Food courts, Kiosks etc.

15) What is Take away point?

The food order is placed at one point and the food is collected and taken away from the premises for the consumption.

16) What is Vending machine service?

This form of service involves a vending machine. The clients make a choice of food and beverages from a selection displayed in the machine. The customer inserts the money to the value of the item chosen. The vending machine can provide food and beverage items hot as well as chilled ranging from snacks to full plated meals.

17) What is In situ/Specialized service?

This form of service happens at areas that are primarily not meant for service.

18) Give few advantages of gueridon service.

- ➢ Brings fame for the outlet
- ➢ Fresh ingredients are used for preparations
- ➢ Staff can exhibit their skills
- ➢ Outlet can earn good profit.

19) Give few disadvantages of gueridon service.

- ➢ Skilled staff required for handling gueridon service
- ➢ Prices of gueridon dishes are relatively higher
- ➢ Gueridon trolley requires more space
- ➢ Carelessness could lead to accidents.

20) Which is the world's first flambé dish and who invented it?

Crêpes Suzette is the world's first flambé dish and Henri Charpentier invented it.

3.5 Cigar, Cigarette & Pipe Tobacco

1) What is Cigar?

Cigar is a tobacco product made from dried and fermented tobacco.

2) What is the shape of a cigar?

A Cigar is mostly cylindrical in shape.

3) Which are the components of a cigar?

Filler (Tripa), Binder (Capote) and Wrapper (Capa).

4) What is 'filler' of a cigar?

Filler is regarded as the heart of a cigar and is made with blend of tobacco leaves. It is responsible for giving a cigar its characteristic flavour and strength. Filler forms the innermost part of a cigar.

5) What is 'binder' of a cigar?

Binders are elastic leaves that hold the filler. It is made of single quality leaf and possesses good tensile strength. A good binder enables the wrapper to burn evenly. Binder normally has little or no flavour at all.

6) What is 'wrapper' of a cigar?

The outermost layer of a cigar is termed as Wrapper and is the key ingredient in determining the cigar's character and flavour. It's the most expensive component (expensive tobacco is used) of a cigar. Wrapper holds the binder and filler intact.

7) Which are the parts of a cigar?

A cigar comprises mainly of 4 parts namely Foot, Body, Band, Head and Cap.

8) What do you mean by the 'ring gauge' of a cigar?

The ring gauge of the cigar actually refers to the diameter of the cigar measured in inches. The diameter of a cigar is measured in 64th of an inch.

9) What is a cigar ring gauge guide?

A cigar ring gauge guide enables a cigar connoisseur to measure the actual ring gauge of a cigar.

10) What is Parejo?

Parejo is the most commonly seen cigar shape and is best identified by its cylindrical body with straight edges.

11) What is Corona?

Corona is a type of Parejo cigar with cylindrical body and straight edges.

12) What is Panatela?

Another kind of Parejo cigar is Panatela which is longer and normally thinner than Coronas.

13) What are Figurado cigars?

Figurado cigars are irregular shaped cigars and are very difficult to manufacture. They are considered as high quality cigars because of the way it is made and generally includes longer and bigger cigars.

14) Give few examples for commonly seen Figurado cigars.

Belicoso, Pyramid, Torpedo, Perfecto, Culebra etc.

15) What is Belicoso cigar?

It is the smallest type of figurado identified by its larger foot and smaller, rounded cap.

16) What is Pyramid cigar?

Pyramid is a kind of figurado cigar best identified by its broad foot and pointed cap.

17) How can you identify a Torpedo cigar?

Though Torpedo is similar to Pyramid by looks, it only tapers off the head and the taper does not extend through the length of the cigar.

18) What is Perfecto?

Perfecto is a cigar which is tapered on both sides. The centre part of the cigar is bulged and the ends are narrow.

19) What is a Culebra cigar?

The term Culebra means 'Snake' in Spanish and refers to three long pointed cigars braided together to form a pretzel shape. Before smoking, they are separated.

20) Classify Cigar based on its colour.

Colour	Denoted as	Meaning
Claro	CCC	Colour varies from light tan to yellowish. Leaves are grown under shade.
Colorado Claro	CC	Medium or mid brown colour. Tobacco of this colour is mostly from Cuba or Dominican Republic. Leaves are exposed to sun.

Colorado/Rosado	C	Dark or Reddish brown colour.
Colorado Maduro	CM	Colorado Maduro is dark brown in colour and the term is related to Honduran or Cuban grown tobacco.
Maduro	M	The colour of this tobacco is exceptionally dark.

21) What is a Cigar menu card?

Cigar menu card is normally offered to customers who visit cigar bars. This menu card features variety of cigars that are available in the cigar bar for purchase. It might have different sections, descriptions for each cigar, size and ring gauge of each cigar along with its price.

22) What is Humidor?

Humidor is a wooden box which is meant for storing cigar and pipe tobacco. This box features a moisture pad which won't let the cigar to go dry and a hygrometer to measure the interior humidity. Humidors hold the cigar at constant temperature and the internal temperature of the box ranges between 68 to 70°F.

23) Is Humidor meant for aging cigar?

No, Humidor is not meant for aging cigar.

24) Why humidors are used?

Humidors are used to store cigars and preserve its colour and aroma.

25) Name the wood widely preferred to make the interior of Humidor.

Spanish cedar wood and Mahogany wood.

26) Which are the different types of humidor?

The different types of humidor are Table, Travel and Room humidor.

27) Name the device that measures the interior humidity of humidor.

Hygrometer.

28) What is a Table humidor?

Table humidor is often seen in a lounge or in the guest room of a house. It can accommodate large no. of cigars and might resemble a teapoy. It features drawers and compartments to store cigars of different sizes and has a glass top.

29) What is a Travel humidor?

This type of humidor is relatively small so that one can easily carry it wherever he goes. Compared to table humidor it is very light and can store 3 to 6 cigars at a time. These days leather travel humidors of varying holding capacities are available in the market.

30) What is Room humidor?

A Room humidor or Walk-in humidor is seen in cigar bars. It's a large room meant for storing cigar with the humidity level rightly maintained. The cigar boxes are kept on wooden racks made of Spanish cedar or Mahogany. The temperature of the room is controlled with the help of a thermostat. Room humidor is expensive to construct and requires more space.

31) Name four cigar equipment.

Cigar cutter, Cigar scissors, Humidor, Match box and Ashtray.

32) Mention the names of cigar cutters.

Guillotine cutter (Single and Double blades), Punch and V shaped cutter.

33) Which cigar is regarded as the best quality cigar in the world?

Cuban cigars particularly Cuban Havana cigar.

34) Give the names of few popular Havana cigar brands.

Ramon Allones, Romeo y Julieta, Monte Cristo, Cabanas and H.Upmann.

35) Mention four international brands of cigars.

Davidoff (Dominican Republic), Dunhill (Dominican Republic), Royal Jamaica (Jamaica) and Temple Hall (Jamaica).

36) Mention two Indian brand names of cigars.

Armenteros and Black Tiger.

37) Name the medium strength, hand rolled cigar brand of ITC.

Armenteros.

38) Which cigar brand is known as the 'Rolls Royce of Cigars'?

Gurkha brand.

39) Which is the world's most expensive cigar?

Gurkha's Royal Courtesan. It costs $ 1.36 million per cigar.

40) Which company makes 'His Majesty's Reserve' (HMR) cigar?

Gurkha.

41) What makes 'His Majesty's Reserve' cigar an expensive one?

This category of cigar is produced in limited numbers and feature cigar made from 15 year old Connecticut wrapper leaf and the cigar is infused in Louis XIII Cognac.

42) Define Cigarette.

Cigarette can be defined as a small roll of finely cut tobacco, enclosed in a wrapper of thin paper which is used for smoking purpose.

43) Which are the different types of cigarettes?

Non Filter, Lights, Ultra Lights, Menthol Cigarettes, Novelty Cigarettes etc.

44) What is a Non Filter cigarette?

Non filter cigarettes have the highest tar and nicotine level among other cigarettes. Since they come without any filters, it is more harmful for the human body.

45) What is a Full Flavour cigarette?

Full flavour cigarettes have the second highest level of nicotine and tar. Though they come with filter, it has high potent flavour.

46) What are Lights?

Lights are cigarettes that are easy to smoke as it has got low level of tar and nicotine.

47) What are Ultra Lights?

Ultra Light cigarettes are characterized by extremely low levels of tar and nicotine.

48) What kind of cigarette is Menthol Cigarette?

Menthol cigarettes are cigarettes with compound menthol which gives a minty flavour to the smoker. Menthol cigarettes are found in full flavoured, light and ultra light types as well.

49) What is Roll Your Own (RYO) Cigarette?

As the name suggests, a smoker can make 'Roll Your Own' cigarettes by purchasing cigarette rolling paper and loose tobacco. The tobacco is put in a cigarette paper and rolled with the ends gummed.

50) What are Novelty Cigarettes?

Novelty Cigarettes, also known as e-cigarettes or electronic cigarettes are those cigarettes that do not contain nicotine. They are smokeless and use nicotine in the form of vapours.

51) What are Herbal Cigarettes?

Herbal cigarettes are made of different herbs and do not contain tobacco or nicotine. The herbs that are mostly used are mint, cinnamon and lemongrass.

52) Give two brand names of herbal cigarette.

NTB and Nirdosh are two famous herbal cigarette brands.

53) What is Kretek?

Kretek is a sweet-smelling clove cigarette that originated in Java, Indonesia. These cigarettes are made from a blend of tobacco, cloves with other flavours. It is the most popular form of cigarette in Indonesia.

54) Name three popular brands of Kretek.

Gudang Garam, Jakarta and Wismilak are few brands of Kretek.

55) Name five international brands of cigarettes.

Marlboro (US), Dunhill (UK), Benson & Hedges (UK), Camel (US) and Hope (Japan).

56) Name five Indian brands of cigarettes.

Wills, Bristol, Gold Flake, Charminar and Scissors.

57) The amount of nicotine present in a cigar is equivalent to the amount of nicotine present in three packets of cigarette-True or False

True.

58) Name the component present in cigar and cigarette that may cause addiction among smokers.

Nicotine.

59) What is the purpose of having filter in cigarettes?

The filter present in cigarettes reduces harshness and brings down the amount of smoke and tar inhaled by the smoker.

60) What is the unique feature of Vantage brand of cigarettes?

The Vantage brand of cigarettes features a special conical hole in the filter that claims to reduce the intake of nicotine and tar by the smoker.

61) Name the mascot used by the Camel cigarette brand which gained wide popularity among smokers.

Joe Camel.

62) Which cigarette brand is named after the town where the owner of the brand was initially working?

Winston.

63) 'Force No Friend, Fear No Foe.' Name the cigarette brand that featured this motto.

Winfield.

64) What is Pipe tobacco?

Pipe tobacco is a kind of dried tobacco used in a pipe to smoke.

65) What is 'pipe' in pipe tobacco?

'Pipe' in pipe tobacco refers to the smoking equipment used by the smoker.

66) How pipe tobacco is different from other forms of tobacco products?

Tobacco used in pipe is given special attention during its making and is blended in a unique way to acquire flavour. It's available in different flavours, sizes, shapes and is found to be less mild than the tobacco used in cigarette.

67) Name three types of Pipe tobacco.

Virginia tobacco, Burley tobacco and Spice tobacco.

68) What is Virginia pipe tobacco?

Virginia pipe tobacco is a flue-cured tobacco which hails from Virginia and is believed to be the most famous pipe tobacco till date. Since it possesses high level of natural sugar content, it leaves sweet taste on the palate of the smoker.

69) What is Virginia Bright?

Virginia Bright is regarded as the best grade of Virginia tobacco.

70) What is Burley tobacco?

The second most popular tobacco after Virginia tobacco is Burley tobacco. It has zero sugar content.

CHAPTER-4

Food

Section no.	Sub-heading	Questions
4.1	Accompaniments	50
4.2	Caviar	20
4.3	Cheese	120
4.4	Indian Sweets	65
4.5	Pasta	60
4.6	Salad	75
4.7	Sauce	35
4.8	Soup	90

4.1 Accompaniments

1) What are Accompaniments?

Accompaniments mainly in the form of sauces, dressings, seasonings and toasts enhances the flavour and balance the taste of the food items with which it is served. It also provides a contrast of texture or helps counteract the richness of food items.

2) What are the objectives of accompaniments?

- To enhance the flavour and balance the taste of the food items

- To provide a contrast of texture of food items.

3) How accompaniments are generally offered?

Accompaniments can be offered in sauce boats, nappy bowls or small bowls, plates, bottles or jars.

4) What is a Cruet set?

Cruet set comprises of salt cellar and pepper caster.

5) Can mustard pot be included in cruet set?

Yes.

6) What are the components of 4 piece cruet set?

Salt cellar, pepper caster, balsamic vinegar and olive oil.

7) What is Sugar dredger?

Sugar dredger is a dispenser with holes used for caster sugar.

8) What is Oyster cruet set?

Oyster cruet set comprises of condiments such as cayenne pepper, pepper mill, chilli vinegar and tabasco sauce.

9) What are the components of Chinese cruet set?

Chilli vinegar, chilli sauce and soya sauce.

10) What is Oriental salt?

A mixture of 1 part of cayenne pepper and 4 parts of salt.

11) Give the accompaniment for Canapé.

Sauces and dips based on the topping.

12) What are the accompaniments for cocktail de pamplemousee and cocktail de florida?

Caster sugar.

13) What is the cover and accompaniment for cocktail de crevettes?

Cover- Cocktail glass, doily on B&B plate, teaspoon and oyster fork.

Accompaniments- Brown bread and butter, cayenne pepper and pepper mill.

14) Give the accompaniment for Maïs Natural/Corn on the cob.

Melted butter and Pepper mill.

15) What are the accompaniments for Pâté de foie gras/ Goose Liver Paste?

Segments of orange and Melba toast/hot breakfast toast with crusts removed and served in a napkin on a B&B plate.

16) What are the accompaniments and cover for Pâté maison?

Accompaniments-Hot toast with crust removed, cut into triangular shape and offered in a B&B plate.

Cover- Side knife, dessert fork and cold fish plate.

17) Give the accompaniments of Melon frappe.

Caster sugar and ground ginger.

18) What are the accompaniments for juices?

It is caster sugar. For tomato juice, Worcestershire sauce and salt is also served.

19) Mention the accompaniments of Smoked salmon.

Lemon wedges, cayenne pepper, pepper mill, brown bread, oil, chopped onions and capers.

20) What is the cover for thick and puree soups?

Soup plate, underliner and soup spoon.

21) Name two soups that have cheese straw as its accompaniment.

Potage Germiny and Turtle soup.

22) What is the general accompaniment for puree soups?

Croutons.

23) Are croutons served with cream soups?

Yes.

24) Name the soup for which sour cream, bouchees filled with duck pate and beetroot juice are served as accompaniments.

Bortsch.

25) What are the accompaniments for omelette?

Bread toast, grilled tomato, hash brown potato and tomato ketchup.

26) What are the accompaniments for Macaroni?

Melted cheese and pasta sauce.

27) Give the accompaniment for Gnocchi, Ravioli and Spaghetti.

Grated parmesan cheese.

28) What is the accompaniment for chow mein?

Soya sauce.

29) What are the accompaniments for different fish preparations?

Fried	Tartar sauce, Remoulade sauce, Gribiche sauce and segments of lemon.
Grilled	If served hot-Béarnaise sauce and Tyrolienne sauce. If served cold-Tartar sauce, Remoulade sauce, Gribiche sauce, segments of lemon.
Poached	If served hot-Hollandaise sauce, Mousseline sauce, Beurre fondue. If served cold-Tartar sauce, Remoulade sauce, Gribiche sauce, segments of lemon.

30) What is the accompaniment of batter fried fish?

Tomato sauce and segments of lemon

31) Give the accompaniment of blue trout.

Melted butter, hollandaise sauce and segments of lemon

32) What are the accompaniments for steak?

French or English mustard, brown sauce, béarnaise sauce, baked jacketed potatoes etc.

33) What is the accompaniment of broiled beef?

Mustard sauce and ketchup.

34) What are the accompaniments for different roasted meat preparations?

Roast Beef	Horse radish sauce, French and English mustard, Yorkshire pudding
Roast Chicken	Bread sauce, Parsley and thyme stuffing, Sage and onion stuffing
Roast Duck	Apple sauce, Sage and onion stuffing
Roast Goose	Apple sauce, Sage and onion stuffing
Roast Lamb	Mint sauce and Onion sauce
Roast Mutton	Red currant jelly and White onion sauce
Roast Pork	Apple sauce, Sage and onion stuffing
Roast Turkey	Cranberry sauce, savoury herb or chestnut stuffing and chipolatas, Game chips, Watercress
Roast Veal	Parsley and thyme stuffing
Roast wild duck	Apple sauce, Sage and onion stuffing

Roast gravy is also served with all roasted meat items.

35) Give the accompaniments for vegetables served hot and cold.

Hot-Hollandaise and melted butter.

Cold-Mayonnaise and vinaigrette sauce.

36) What are the accompaniments for cold meats?

Chutney, mustard and relishes.

37) Give the accompaniment for cold lobster.

Mayonnaise sauce and segments of lemon.

38) What are the accompaniments offered for cheese on a cheese board?

Almonds, celery sticks, cruet set, cheese crackers, cured meat, honey, radish sticks etc.

39) Name three accompaniments served with savoury food items

Cayenne pepper, pepper mill and Worcestershire sauce.

40) Give the accompaniment for waffles.

Different syrups, honey, jam and jellies.

41) What are the accompaniments for fruits?

Caster sugar, cream and sweet sauces.

42) What is the accompaniment for nuts?

Salt.

43) What is the accompaniment for hot chocolate?

Whipped cream.

44) Name few condiments served in fast food outlets as accompaniments.

Sauce, mustard, ketchup and mayonnaise.

45) Give the description for the following accompaniments

Accompaniment	Description
Apple sauce	A sauce made with Apple puree, cinnamon powder, butter, sugar and water. Traditional accompaniment of Roast Duck.
Balsamic vinegar	A thick, sweet smelling vinegar made from the pure and unfermented juice of grape
Béarnaise sauce	Clarified butter and egg yolks flavored with tarragon and shallots, with chervil and tarragon simmered in vinegar to make a reduction.
Blinis	A small savoury pancake served with Caviar. Russian origin and is made from leavened bread.
Bread sauce	Flavoured milk with onions +bread crumbs +butter + cream + seasoning.
Caper sauce	Made from caper plant along with its bud and fruits.
Cayenne Pepper	Very strong pepper obtained from dried, ground red chillies. It's from Cayenne, city in French Guyana. Also known as Red Pepper.
Chives	Herb
Crackers	Thin flaky dry biscuits eaten with cheese.
Cranberry Sauce	A sauce made from red berries and is the traditional accompaniment of Roast Turkey
Croutons	A small piece of bread or toasted bread served with a soup or used as a garnish.
Cumberland sauce	Fruit based sauce made from red currants, port or wine, mustard, pepper, orange, ginger and vinegar.
English Mustard	Yellow condiment made from a mixture of black and white mustard.
French Mustard	Pungent mustard made from black or brown mustard seeds.

Game chips	Thin crisp chips (potato) are usually served with game dishes
Gribiche sauce	Gribiche is made with shallots, parsley, cornichons, capers, eggs, oil, vinegar, seasonings chives, other herbs and prepared mustard.
Grilled Flute	A thin slice of French bread weighing 100 gms, grilled and served before service.
Hollandaise sauce	A rich creamy sauce made of butter, egg yolks, and lemon juice or vinegar.
Horseradish Sauce	Made from the root of the horseradish plant. It's grated, boiled, reduced, strained and finished with mustard and egg yolks. It's the accompaniment of Roast Beef.
Mayonnaise sauce	An emulsion of raw egg yolks, salad/olive oil, vinegar and mustard powder with seasonings. A cold sauce.
Melba Toast	Very thin slices of bread with one side of the crust cut, before it is toasted.
Mousseline sauce	Hollandaise sauce containing whipped cream.
Red Currant Jelly	A jelly made from red currant berries, traditionally served with Roast Mutton.
Remoulade sauce	A sauce very similar to Tartar sauce, yellowish colour, Mayonnaise +Chopped pickles+ horseradish, paprika+ anchovies+ capers and a host of other items.
Roast Gravy	It's made from meat juices which congeal and caramelize in the bottom of a roasting pan. For red meat, the gravy should be dark brown and for lighter meats it should be golden brown. For increasing the flavour of Roast gravy, onion, carrot and a mixture of stock and wine are boiled and reduced. Later it's strained and seasoned.
Tabasco Sauce	A pungent, pepper sauce made from Tabasco chilli pepper, from West Indies.

Continued…

Tartar sauce	Mayonnaise +chopped pickles+ olives+ capers.
Truffles	Edible mushrooms found underground especially near the roots of oak trees.
Tyrolienne sauce	Béarnaise sauce+ Butter.
Vinaigrette Dressing	A cold sauce made from vinegar, oil, pepper and salt. It's used as a dressing for salads.
Watercress	Green leafy vegetable with small round leaves with a pungent flavour.
Worcestershire Sauce	Spicy sauce made from vinegar, molasses, sugar and spices.
Yorkshire Pudding	Traditional accompaniment of Roast Beef. Made from a batter of flour, eggs and milk and is baked in an oven.

46) What is Chutney?

An Indian relish made from fruits or vegetables by mixing it with vinegar, sugar and spices is termed as Chutney. The addition of spices and chillies makes it spicy. Examples are mango chutney and date chutney.

47) What are Pickles?

Pickles are vegetables or fruits preserved in solution of either brine or vinegar. Gherkins and cucumber are two vegetables that are pickled.

48) What are Preserves?

Preserves are condiments used as spreads and are made by preserving fruits in sugar or acid. Jams and jellies fall under this category.

49) What are Relishes?

The term relish refers to a type of condiment made by cutting vegetables and fruits into fine pieces, preserving it in either vinegar or sugar. Relishes can be sweet, sour, spicy or a mixed flavour and counteract the richness of food items. Examples are Indian raitha, chutney, kimchi and sambal.

50) What is Sambal?

An Indonesian and Malaysian relish which is spicy in nature, generally offered as a side dish is Sambal.

4.2 Caviar

1) What is Caviar?

Caviar refers to the roe (eggs) of sturgeon fish which are of great demand.

2) Name the nations that are involved in caviar trade (bordering Caspian Sea).

Russia, Iran, Turkmenistan, Kazakhstan and Azerbaijan.

3) Name three main types of Caviar from Caspian Sea

Names	Colour	Size	Other features
Sevruga	Steel-grey	Small	Abundant
Beluga	Golden-grey	Large	Rare and High demand
Osetra/Asetra	Golden brown	Medium	-

4) Which variety of caviar is the largest?

Beluga.

5) Which type of caviar is regarded as best quality caviar?

Beluga.

6) Name the smallest type of caviar.

Sevruga.

7) What is 'True Caviar'?

Fish roe (eggs) obtained from Beluga, Osetra and Sevruga sturgeon is considered as 'true' caviar.

8) Name the additives of Caviar.

Salt and Borax.

9) What is the purpose of adding Borax to salted Caviar in Russia?

It is done traditionally as Borax acts as a sweetener and aids in preserving Caviar

10) Name the country where addition of Borax to Caviar is considered illegal

United States.

11) What do you mean by 'Malossol' Caviar?

The term 'Malossol' is used to refer caviar with low salt content.

12) Why metallic or silver spoons are not used while serving Caviar?

Metallic or silver spoons are generally avoided while serving Caviar as it imparts metallic flavour to caviar and tarnishes the spoon.

Spoons used in its service are made from horn, wood, bone, tortoise shell and mother-of-pearl

13) Can caviar be served from its original tin?

Yes.

14) What is the serving temperature of caviar?

22.2°C (28°F).

15) Give the features of traditional caviar tins that come from Russia.

If the lid of the caviar tin has blue circle it indicates that it is Beluga caviar, yellow rim indicates that it is osetra and red rim indicates that it is sevruga.

16) Which is the classic pair for Caviar?

Champagne as its acidity can moderate the saltiness of caviar.

17) What are the accompaniments of Caviar?

Melba toast, blinis, butter, segments of lemon, sieved hard boiled yolk and white of egg, chopped shallots, capers, parsley etc.

18) What is the cover for caviar?

The cover includes caviar/side/fish knife and cold fish plate.

19) What is the shelf life of an opened jar or tin of caviar?

The quality of caviar starts deteriorating once the jar or tin of caviar is opened. Hence, it should be consumed within two to three days.

20) Name caviar infused vodka.

L'Orbe.

4.3 Cheese

1) What is Cheese?

Cheese is a nutritious food made from milk.

2) Why cheese is regarded as a nutritious food?

Cheese is said to be a nutritious food since it has protein, vitamins, calcium and phosphorous.

3) From which Latin word did the word cheese originate?

The word cheese originated from the Latin word, 'caseus'.

4) Name the major ingredients used in cheese making

Milk, Rennet and Microbes (good bacteria).

5) What is the role of cheese in the food industry?

Cheese itself is a food and is also used extensively in cooking, for preparing sauces (Mornay sauce), soups (French Onion Soup), fondue (Gouda), salads (Italian Salad) and bakery products (Cheese Cake).

6) Who is a cheese monger?

Cheese monger is a person who sells cheese and other milk products.

7) Classify cheese.

Cheese is classified on the basis of its country of origin, source, rind, colour, texture and shape.

8) Give examples for cheese based on country of origin

Name of the cheese	*Country*
Brie, Camembert, Roquefort, Munster	France
Gorgonzola, Parmigiano Reggiano, Provolone, Mozzarella	Italy
Stilton, Cornish Blue, Caerphilly, Cheddar	England
Emmentaler, Gruyère, Formaggini, Vacherin	Switzerland (Swiss)
Danish Blue, Danbo, Samsoe, Danish Tilsit	Netherlands (Denmark)
Harzer, Mainzer, Quark, Korbkäse	Germany
Paneer, Khoya, Bandel, Kalari	India

9) Give examples for cheese based on its source

Name of the cheese	*Source*
Brie, Camembert, Gorgonzola	Cow's milk
Mozzarella di Bufala, Stracciatella di Bufala	Buffalo's milk
Chévre, Goat Brie, Nababbo	Goat's milk
Roquefort, Ricotto, Feta	Sheep's milk
Rajya Metok and Chhurpi	Yak's milk

10) Give examples for cheese based on its rind

Name of the cheese	*Rind*
Brie	White rind
Edam	Rind of red paraffin wax
Emmentaler	Thin rind
Gouda	Brown rind
Feta	No rind

11) Give examples for cheese based on its colour

Name of the cheese	Colour
Cheddar	Orange
Emmentaler	Ivory yellow
Feta	White

12) Give examples for cheese based on its texture

Name of the cheese	Texture
Cheddar, Parmesan, Stilton	Hard
Edam, Gouda, Gruyère	Semi-hard
Brie, Camembert, Valençay	Soft
Mascarpone, Mozzarella, Ricotta	Fresh

13) Give examples for cheese based on its shape

Name of the cheese	Shape
Cheddar	Round
Parmesan	Drum
Roquefort	Cylinder
Sainte-Maure de Touraine	Log
Valençay	Pyramid

14) Name a cheese which is made from partially skimmed cow's milk.

Parmigiano Reggiano.

15) Name one cheese which is used in baking.

Gruyère from Switzerland.

16) Name two cheese varieties that are used as topping.

Mozzarella and Parmesan.

17) Give the names of two cheeses used in cooking.

Ricotta and Mozzarella.

18) Name one cheese used in making salads.

Parmigiano Reggiano.

19) Name the leading cheese producer of the world.

USA.

20) Name two cheeses with geographical indication status.

Parmigiano Reggiano of Italy and Roquefort of France.

21) Which cheese from Cyprus had received protected status from European Union recently?

Halloumi.

22) Who were the first to develop the art of cheese making?

The Romans.

23) Name the special kitchen used by the Romans for preparing cheese.

Careale.

24) Name the animals whose milk is commonly used in cheese making.

Cow, Goat, Sheep and Buffalo.

25) Why horse's milk is not used for making cheese?

It is not used since it has low milk protein.

26) Name one brand of cheese made from camel's milk

Caravane (Mauritania).

27) Which cheese bears the nickname 'Camelbert Cheese?'

Caravane.

28) Give two examples for Yak cheese.

Rajya Metok (Tibet) and Chhurpi (Nepal).

29) Name the country which produces cheese from the milk of moose.

Sweden.

30) Why few big cheeses are 'wheel' shaped?

Few big cheeses are 'wheel' shaped since it is easy to be rolled from one place to the other.

31) Which are the parts of cheese?

Rind and Paste.

32) What is Rind?

Rind is the outer (visible) part of a cheese.

33) Are all rinds edible?

No, not all rinds are edible.

34) How the rinds develop?

Rinds on cheese develop during its ripening process as a result of humidity and temperature conditions along with the reaction of molds on the surface of cheese.

35) What are Natural rinds?

Rinds that form on the exterior of cheese naturally are termed as Natural rinds.

36) Give two examples for cheese with natural rind.

Caerphilly and Stilton.

37) What are Washed rinds?

The affineur (master in cheese making) sprays a solution (either brine or alcohol or a combination of both) on the top part of the cheese so that it provides a suitable environment for edible moulds to grow.

38) Give two examples for cheese with washed rind.

Stinking Bishop (UK) and Limburger (Limburg).

39) What is the purpose of having waxed rind for few cheeses?

The waxed rind protects the cheese from the development of unwanted mold on the exterior of cheese and at the same time retains the moisture content during the ripening of cheese.

40) Name two cheeses with waxed rind.

Edam and Gouda.

41) What is Paste?

The interior part of a cheese is known as Paste and is edible.

42) How cheese gets its colour?

It could happen naturally or by the addition of natural food dyes or by injecting 'Pencillium' molds.

43) Which pigment gives the buttery yellow colour to cheese?

Beta carotene.

44) What gives orange colour to cheeses such as Cheddar and Colby?

A seed named annatto (its pigment bixin gives colour).

45) What is Rennet?

Rennet is an enzyme used to coagulate milk for making cheese.

46) Name two important enzymes present in Rennet.

Chymotrypsin and Pepsin.

47) What is Rennin (Chymosin)?

Rennin is a type of enzyme which is present is Rennet.

48) Where is Rennet present?

Rennet is present in the stomach of young mammals like calf.

49) Name the milk protein which gets coagulated by the addition of rennet.

Casein.

50) What is Vegetable Rennet?

Vegetable Rennet is a type of rennet obtained from plant sources. It is used to coagulate milk for making cheese for the vegans.

51) Give one example for Vegetable Rennet.

Flowers of wild cardoon thistle are used to make Vegetable Rennet.

52) Which term is used to denote the 'holes' in a cheese?

Eyes.

53) What are cheeses without 'eyes' called?

Blind.

54) Name one well known cheese from France.

Brie.

55) Name the cheese which is often referred to as "King of Cheeses".

Parmigiano Reggiano from Italy.

56) Name the "King of English Cheeses".

Blue Stilton.

57) Which blue veined cheese is known as "King of Cheeses" in France?

Roquefort.

58) Which cheese is often referred as the "Queen of Cheeses"?

Brie.

59) Which Italian cheese comes in the shape of sausage/pear/cone?

Provolone Valdapana.

60) Name a cheese from Greece.

Feta.

61) Which are the types of Brie Cheese?

Brie de Meaux and Brie de Melun.

62) Name two popular cheeses from California.

Monterey Jack and Red Hawk.

63) Name the cheese used in famous Italian dessert, Tiramisu.

Mascarpone.

64) What type of cheese is Mascarpone?

Mascarpone is a cream cheese.

65) What is Ricotta?

Ricotta is an Italian cheese made from whey.

66) What is the meaning of the word 'Ricotta'?

Ricotta means 'cooked again' or 're-cooked'.

67) Name two cheeses made without the addition of rennet.

Ricotta (Italy) and Paneer (India).

68) What is Paneer?

Paneer is a type of cottage cheese produced in India.

69) What is Cottage cheese?

Cottage cheese is a type of fresh cheese made by mixing cream with skimmed milk curds.

70) Name few cheeses made from whey

Ricotta (Italy), Manouri (Greece), Gjetost (Norway) etc.

71) Name the queen who received a big, round wheel of Cheddar cheese as a wedding present.

Queen Victoria.

72) Which cheese is named after a city in Netherlands?

Gouda.

73) What is the difference between Parmigiano Reggiano and Parmesan?

Parmigiano Reggiano is a famous hard cheese from Italy whereas Parmesan is a generic term often used outside EU to denote cheeses made in the style of 'Parmigiano Reggiano'.

74) Which cheese was once offered as food to the coal miners?

Caerphilly.

75) Name the cheese which bears the nick name 'The Crumblies'.

Caerphilly.

76) Which cheese is known as 'Parmesan of Mexico'?

Cotija.

77) How Brick cheese got its name?

Brick cheese is named so since real bricks were used to press the cheese.

78) What is Processed cheese?

Processed cheese is a variety of cheese made by mixing cheese with emulsifiers and stabilizers. It is then melted by heat and is cut either in triangular or cube shape and is covered with a foil.

79) What kinds of cheeses are referred to as 'artisan' cheeses?

The term 'artisan' is used to refer cheeses that are made in the traditional way and are often manufactured in small batches.

80) What is a Cheese spread?

It is a form of processed cheese used as a spread mainly for breads, burger buns and sandwiches.

81) Name the world's costliest cheese.

'Pule' made from donkey's milk is the world's costliest cheese.

82) Discuss one unique feature of Swiss cheese.

Swiss cheese is a kind of cheese manufactured in Switzerland and is best identified by the 'holes' present in it.

83) How Swiss cheese get holes in it?

The bacteria present in the cheese releases carbon dioxide gas which eventually creates holes in it. A recent study says that the holes are created because of the hay particles which are present in milk.

84) Name the bacteria used in making Emmentaler cheese.

P.Shermanii.

85) Give one example for a popular Swiss cheese.

Emmentaler/Emmental.

86) Name the cheese that is featured in the famous Tom and Jerry cartoon.

Emmental from Switzerland.

87) Give two examples for cheese that has holes (eyes) in it.

Emmental from Switzerland and St.Claire from Tasmania.

88) Name the most 'smelliest' cheese in the world.

Vieux-Boulogne from France.

89) Which cheese's smell is compared to the smell of sweaty feet?

Limburger.

90) Name the cheese which is banned from public transport in France due to its smell.

Epoisses de Bourgogne.

91) What is so unique about 'Sage Derby' cheese?

'Sage Derby' cheese is identified by its mottled green colour.

92) Name the cheese that contains maggots (larva of fly).

Casu Marzu from Sardinia, Italy.

94) What is a Cheese board?

Cheese board serves the purpose of presentation of cheese. Different types of cheeses are displayed along with its traditional accompaniments and equipments. The board is also used to cut the cheese according to the needs of the diner.

95) What is a Cheese spray?

A Cheese spray is a form of processed cheese in a squeezable tube with a cap and nozzle. It was designed to make the cheese readily available to the person who requires it.

96) What is Cheese fondue?

Cheese fondue is a hot cheese preparation made with melted cheese, garlic, white wine, corn flour and cherry brandy. The fondue is kept on a pan and is placed on a table for the guests.

97) Name the special equipment used to insert bread cubes to dip them in fondue.

Fondue fork.

98) What are cheese straws?

Cheese pastry cut into finger like strips are known as Cheese straws.

99) What is Leipäjuusto?

It's a Finnish cheese made from cow's milk. The word 'Leipäjuusto' literally means bread cheese.

100) Name few accompaniments for cheese

Almonds, Cheese crackers, Radish, Olives, Carrot, Cured meat etc.

101) Which are the most commonly used herbs in cheese making?

Tarragon, Marjoram and Rosemary.

102) Name few equipment used in the service of cheese

Cheese fork, cheese knife, cheese wire cutter, cheese cleaver, cheese plane, cuore knife etc.

103) What is Blue cheese?

Blue cheese is a kind of cheese which is made by inducing a mould called 'Pencillium.'

104) Which animal's milk is generally used to make blue cheese?

Cow's milk.

105) Name few popular varieties of blue cheese.

Stilton, Gorgonzola, Roquefort etc.

106) How blue veined cheeses get its colour?

It is because of the penicillin culture which is injected to the cheese.

107) Name the penicillin culture used in Roquefort cheese.

Penicillium Roqueforti.

108) Name the cheese which is aged in natural Combalou caves of Roquefort-sur-Soulzon.

Roquefort.

109) Name the man who had set the standards for Stilton cheese.

Frances Pawlett.

110) Name the author who gave the title 'the English Parmesan' to Stilton cheese.

Defoe.

111) Which inn popularized the trade of Stilton cheese?

The Bell Inn.

112) Which are the two types of Stilton Cheese?

Stilton Blue and Stilton White.

113) How Stilton cheese came to be associated with Christmas in Britain?

The Stilton cheese preparation starts at the end of summer from the best quality milk and is ready right in time for Christmas.

114) Name the oldest blue cheese in the world.

Gorgonzola from Italy.

115) What is Limburger?

A cow's milk based cheese with strong flavor from Liège of Belgium.

116) What is the term used to denote a cheese lover?

Turophile.

117) Why certain cheeses feature wood ash in its exterior surface?

For years this process is carried out to ensure that the cheese is not getting spoiled due to excess moisture and creates a favourable environment for the beneficial mold to bloom.

118) Give few points pertaining to the storage of cheese.

- Cheese should be kept wrapped and shouldn't be too much exposed to cold and heat

- Store the cheese in the fridge in its original wrapper.

- Avoid stacking the cheese on top of each other as this could damage the rind.

- Store cheese away from strong smelling food items.

119) Name four cheeses that could be aged.

Cheddar, Manchego, Gorgonzola and Gouda.

120) What is the difference between an affineur and turophile?

An affineur is regarded as an expert in aging cheese whereas a turophile/caseophile is a person who loves cheese.

4.4 Indian Sweets

1) What are Indian Sweets (Mithai)?

The term Indian Sweets or 'Mithai' refer to various sweet delicacies prepared in India. They are mostly milk and sugar based preparations that might have originated as part of Indian culture and tradition.

2) Classify Indian sweets.

Indian sweets are classified into North Indian sweets, South Indian sweets, West Indian sweets and East Indian sweets.

3) What are North Indian sweets?

Indian sweets which are indigenous to northern part of India i.e., Jammu & Kashmir, Himachal Pradesh, Uttar Pradesh, Madhya Pradesh, Gujarat, Rajasthan, Bihar, Punjab, Delhi, Chandigarh, Haryana, Uttarakhand etc.

4) Give few examples for famous North Indian sweet delicacies.

Shufta (Jammu & Kashmir), Kalakand (Rajasthan) Rasgulla (Bengal) and Sandesh (Bengal).

5) Give few examples for South Indian sweet dishes.

Chiroti (Karnataka), Payasam (Kerala), Mysore Pak (Mysore) and Pakundalu (Andhra Pradesh).

6) Name three milk based Indian sweet preparations.

Rabri, Rasmalai and Kalakand.

7) What is Rasmalai?

Balls of paneer soaked in sweetened, thickened, flavoured milk.

8) What does the word 'rasmalai' mean?

The word 'ras' means juice and 'malai' means cream.

9) What is Sandesh?

Sandesh is a sweet preparation from Bengal which is made from milk and sugar.

10) Which Indian sweet means 'message' in Bengali language?

Sandesh.

11) Which Indian sweet is also referred to as 'Badushah'?

Balushahi.

12) Name the traditional sweet prepared in Andhra Pradesh during Makarasankranti festival.

Pakundalu.

13) Name the traditional sweet associated with Onam, the harvest festival of Kerala.

Payasam.

14) What is Jalebi?

Jalebi is a popular Indian sweet made by deep frying all purpose flour batter into circular shapes. It can be served cold or warm.

15) What is Imarti?

Lentil batter is deep fried and soaked in sugar syrup, flavored with cardamom and rose essence to prepare Imarti.

16) What is Kheer?

Kheer is a milk based rice pudding.

17) What are the different types of kheer preparations?

Badam kheer, Paneer kheer, Rice kheer, Soya kheer etc.

18) What is Phirni?

Phirni is an exotic sweet preparation similar to kheer from Kashmir.

19) Differentiate Kheer from Phirni.

Criteria of differentiation	*Kheer*	*Phirni*
Consistency	Thin	Thick
Type of rice used	Whole rice	Ground rice
Serving temperature	Warm as well as chilled	Chilled

20) What is Basundi?

Basundi is milk based sweet preparation with cardamom and dry fruits.

21) Basundi is generally served with a deep fried Indian bread. Identify it.

Puri.

22) What is Halva?

Halva meaning 'sweet' in India refers to either flour or nut based preparation sweetened with sugar.

23) Which is the most important ingredient in halva?

Ghee.

24) What is the garnish used for halva?

Nuts.

25) Name few nuts used in halva.

Badam, Cashew nuts, Pine nuts and Pistachio.

26) Can Halva be served cold?

No, it should be served warm.

27) Which is the most popular type of halva across India?

Semolina based halva.

28) Give few examples for Halva preparations.

Gajar ka halva, Sooji halva, Kashi halva

29) Who is 'halvai'?

Halvai is a term used to denote the person who prepares sweets/ mithai.

30) What is Gulab jamun?

Fried dough (Khoa) balls soaked in rose flavoured sugar syrup.

31) What does the term Gulab jamun mean?

It means rose berries-Gulab means 'rose' and Jamun means 'berries' in Hindi.

32) How Gulab jamun got its name?

Since the size of fried khoa balls is similar to jamun berries and is soaked in rose flavoured sugar syrup, hence the name.

33) How Gulab jamun should be served?

It could be served either warm or cold.

34) What is Bebinca?

A Goan sweet delicacy made using butter, coconut milk, eggs, flour and nutmeg is Bebinca.

35) Traditionally speaking, how many layers are seen in Bebinca?

Seven layers.

36) Name the 'Queen of Goan desserts'.

Bebinca.

37) Which is the traditional earthenware oven used to bake Bebinca?

Tizals.

38) Which is the square shaped sweet preparation made using groundnuts and jaggery?

Chikki.

39) Which sweet delicacy means 'royal piece'?

Shahi Tukda.

40) What is Shahi Tukda?

Shahi Tukda is a famous Mughalai bread pudding preparation made with ghee, sweetened milk, cardamom, saffron and garnished with nuts.

41) Why people consume Shahi Tukda in fewer quantities?

As the calorific value of Shahi Tukda is high, people consume it in fewer quantities.

42) What is Rajbhog?

Rajbhog is a sweet delicacy from Bengal and is saffron flavoured paneer stuffed with dry fruits. It's a popular variant of Rasgulla.

43) What is Ladoo/Laddu?

A ball shaped sweet preparation made from flour, fat and sugar is Ladoo.

44) Name few varieties of ladoos

Motichoor ka ladoo, Gond ke ladoo, Malai ke ladoo, Rava ladoo etc.

45) What is Mothi choor ladoo?

Mothi choor ladoo is a variety of ladoo prepared by deep frying small balls of besan in ghee and mixed with sugar syrup.

46) What does the term Mothi choor mean in Hindi?

In Hindi, it means 'crushed pearls'-Mothi means 'pearls' and choor means 'to crush'.

47) Name the Indian sweet which takes its name from the word 'Burf' means 'snow' in Hindi.

Burfi.

48) What is Burfi?

Burfi is an Indian mithai prepared from condensed milk, ghee and sugar.

49) Give few examples for burfi.

Badam burfi, Kaaju burfi, Rava burfi,

50) Name the edible silver leaf used to cover burfi and other sweets.

Vark.

51) What is the role of silver paper/leaf in sweets?

The silver paper avoids oxidation of fat while preparing sweets and at the same time improves the overall appearance of the sweets. Moreover, the silver paper keeps the sweets safe from microbial contamination.

52) What is Peda?

An Indian sweet preparation made by combining milk solids, sugar, saffron, cardamom and pistachio nuts is Peda.

53) Name the birthplace of Peda.

Mathura, Uttar Pradesh.

54) What is Modak?

A Maharashtrian sweet, stuffed dumpling made from rice flour dough is Modak.

55) Name the Indian sweet prepared at homes in Maharashtra during Vinayaka chathurthi.

Modak.

56) Which Rajasthani sweet preparation is a maida based, disc shaped cake?

Ghevar.

57) Name the 'Royal Sweet of Mysore'.

Mysore Pak.

58) What is Mysore Pak?

Mysore Pak is a sweet delicacy from Mysore made by combining three ingredients-besan, ghee and sugar.

59) Name the 'King of Indian sweets'.

Rosogolla.

60) Name the 'Queen of Indian sweets'.

Jalebi.

61) Give three examples for Indian sweets that have GI (Geographical Indication) status.

Dharwad Peda (Karnataka, got the status in 2007)

Rosogolla (West Bengal, got the status in 2017)

Kovilpatti Kadalai Mittai (Tamilnadu, got the status in 2020)

62) What are Indian sweetmeats?

The term Indian sweetmeats refer to Indina food preparations rich in sugar.

63) Why sweets are consumed at the end of a meal?

When a person is having his meal, the spicy food items activate his digestive juices in the stomach. When he is consuming sweets at the end of his meal the process stops.

64) Give the names of few Indian sweets along with its region.

Name of the sweet	*Region*
Shufta	Jammu & Kashmir
Gond ke Ladoo	Haryana
Anarsa	Jharkhand
Balushahi	Uttar Pradesh
Chehena Poda	Orissa
Mawa Bati	Madhya Pradesh
Rosogolla	West Bengal
Ghevar	Rajasthan
Pinni	Punjab
Mohanthal	Gujarat
Bebinca	Goa
Modak	Maharashtra
Mysore Pak	Karnataka
Illayappam	Kerala
Khubani ka Meetha	Andhra Pradesh
Khaja	Bihar
Chakarai Pongal	Tamil Nadu

65) Which sweet is regarded as the 'National sweet of India'?

Jalebi.

4.5 Pasta-Anything is Pastable

1) What is Pasta?

Pasta is wheat based dough which is formed into various shapes, boiled and eaten.

2) Where was Pasta invented?

Italy /China.

3) Name the Arab precursor of Pasta.

Itriyya.

4) What is the meaning of the word 'pasta'?

Pasta means 'barley porridge' in Greek, 'dough pastry cake' in Latin and 'paste' in Italian.

5) Which country is the largest consumer of Pasta?

Italy.

6) When is 'World Pasta Day' observed?

On 25th of October, each year.

7) Where is the 'Museum of Pasta' located?

The 'Museum of Pasta' is located in the Province of Parma, Italy.

8) What are the ingredients used to prepare pasta?

Flour (made from durum wheat), water, eggs and olive oil.

9) Give some additional ingredients used in the preparation of pasta.

Bay leaf, celery, garlic, salt etc.

10) What are the different types of flour used in pasta making?

Durum wheat flour, buckwheat flour, refined flour, semolina etc.

11) Why durum wheat flour is the most preferred flour to make pasta?

Because of its high gluten content, the pasta maker can stretch and make more shapes out of it.

12) How many shapes of pasta exist?

According to International Pasta Organisation, more than 600 shapes of pasta exist in the world.

13) Which are the different types of pasta?

Dry (Pasta Secca) and Fresh (Pasta Fresca).

14) Mention two examples for dry pasta.

Spaghetti and Vermicelli.

15) What is fresh pasta?

Pasta prepared just before cooking it is termed as Fresh pasta.

16) Differentiate dry pasta from fresh pasta.

Criteria of differentiation	*Dry pasta*	*Fresh pasta*
Texture	Rough	Smooth and light.
Calories	More	Low
Perfect pair	Meaty, spicy and oily sauces.	Dairy based sauces.

17) What is the common term used to denote the doneness of pasta?

'Al dente' (means 'to the tooth').

18) Which country introduced pasta machine?

Italy.

19) Name the pasta which literally means 'hollow straws'.

Bucatini.

20) Give few examples for stuffed pasta.

Cappelletti, Ravioli and Tortellini.

21) Which pasta means 'strings'?

Spaghetti.

22) Name the pasta which literally means 'little worms'.

Vermicelli.

23) Which pasta looks similar to spaghetti but is hollow in the centre?

Bucatini.

24) Name the pasta popularly known as Angel hair pasta.

Capellini.

25) Which pasta is the thinnest among string pastas?

Capellini.

26) Name the pasta that has the shape of butterflies.

Farfalle.

27) Which pasta is known as bow-tie pasta?

Farfalle.

28) Give two examples for corkscrew shaped pasta.

Fusilli and Rotini.

29) How pasta gets green and red colour?

The juice of spinach and beetroot is added to pasta to obtain these colours respectively.

30) Which pasta bears the shape of wheel with spokes?

Rotelle.

31) Name the vermicelli look alike pasta used in Italian broths and thin soups.

Filini.

32) Which pasta is known as 'belly button' pasta?

Tortellini.

33) Give two examples for tubular pasta.

Cannelloni and Macaroni.

34) Name the seashell shaped pasta.

Conchiglie.

35) Which pasta literally means 'little ribbons'?

Fettuccine.

36) Name the most famous Fettuccine pasta preparation.

Fettuccine Alfredo.

37) Which pasta comes in sheets of various sizes with ripples on its sides?

Lasagna.

38) What is the purpose of a hole in the centre of spaghetti spoon?

The hole enables the person who is cooking to measure one serving of spaghetti.

39) Name few popular Spaghetti preparations.

- Spaghetti Bolognaise (Spaghetti blended with minced beef in a rich brown sauce).

- Spaghetti Napolitaine (Spaghetti in a tomato and garlic flavoured sauce).

- Spaghetti with meat balls (Spaghetti along with ground meat rolled into ball shape and served with tomato sauce).

40) How can you differentiate linguini from spaghetti?

When compared to spaghetti, linguini is thinner and longer in appearance.

41) Under which course will you serve pasta dishes in a 17 course French classical meal structure?

Course no.4, Farineux in which farinaceous dishes are served.

42) Under which course will you serve pasta dishes in an Italian classical meal structure?

Primi, the first course.

43) Name few pasta sauces.

Alfredo, Bolognese, Pesto, Marinara etc.

44) What is Pesto sauce?

A sauce prepared with basil, garlic and pine nuts.

45) Which sauce is known as the 'angry' pasta sauce?

Arrabbiata.

46) Name two sauces which could be served with spaghetti.

Marinara and Pesto.

47) Name the pasta loved by the famous cartoon character, Garfield.

Lasagna.

48) Which is the most popular macaroni and cheese recipe in US?

Mac 'n' Cheese.

49) What is the shape of Macaroni pasta?

Elbow shaped tubular pasta.

50) Mention two differences between spaghetti and noodles.

Criteria of differentiation	Spaghetti	Noodles
Place of origin	Italy	China
Texture	Heavy	Light

51) Which is the most commonly served accompaniment with pasta dishes?

Grated parmesan cheese.

52) What is the cover for spaghetti and other pasta dishes?

Cover for spaghetti is joint fork on right and sweet spoon on the left. For other pasta dishes, a sweet spoon on the right side and sweet fork on the left side is placed.

53) What is the American and Italian style of eating spaghetti?

Americans use both spoon and fork to consume spaghetti whereas Italians use only fork to eat spaghetti

54) Which pasta has the shape of snail shells?

Lumache/Lumaconi.

55) Name the pasta which literally means 'priest strangler'.

Strozzapreti.

56) Which pasta with the meaning 'little ears' is used in pasta salads?

Orecchiette.

57) Name any two popular varieties of pasta.

Penne and spaghetti.

58) Why there exist so many different shapes for pasta?

Different shapes suit different recipes.

59) Which is the ideal plate to serve pasta?

Pasta plate (8 to 10 inches diameter) or pasta bowls could be used to serve pasta.

60) Why the centre part of pasta plate has a shallow dip?

It gives some height to the rim of the plate thereby creating a good meal experience for the person consuming pasta.

4.6 Salad

1) What is Salad?

Salad is a healthy food that comprises of mixture of different vegetables, meat, fish, seafood, egg, cheese, rice, pasta, fruits and nuts. It's mixed with a dressing before serving. The ingredients used in making salad could be either raw or cooked or combination of both.

2) Who is credited with the invention of salads?

Romans were the first to make salads.

3) Mention the origin of the word 'salad'.

The word 'salad' is taken from the Latin word 'sal' which means 'salted'.

4) What was salad initially called?

Ancient Romans called salad as 'herba salata' which means 'salted greens'.

5) What are the parts/components of a salad?

Base/Underliner (generally a leafy vegetable but these days rice, pasta and even fruits are used), Body (Vegetables/Meat/Fish/Egg/Pasta), Dressing (Vinaigrette/Mayonniase/Acidulated cream) and Garnish (Segments of fruits/nuts).

6) What are the different types of salad?

There are mainly two kinds of salads namely Simple/Plain salads and Mixed/Composite salads.

7) Explain different types of salads with examples.

Simple/Plain salads – Salads with primarily one main ingredient. E.g-Cucumber salad and Beetroot salad.

Mixed/Composite salads – Salads with more than one ingredient. E.g-Caesar salad and Tuna salad.

8) What are Warm Salads/Salades Tièdes?

These are normal salads finished with a warm dressing instead of a cold dressing. They need to be served immediately once prepared as hot horsd'oeuvre. Normally this salad feature fish or meat items. Chicken salad with warm cream and coriander dressing is an example for the same.

9) What is a Bound salad?

Bound salad is a term used to denote salads that are held together with the help of a dressing (generally mayonnaise). Example includes Tuna salad and Egg salad.

10) How salad can be served as a part of a meal?

Salad could be served as a starter, entrée, side dish to a main course and dessert.

11) Give few points that one need to consider if salad is offered as the main course.

- Items rich in protein need to be included in the salad

- For non-vegans, red meat and white meat could be included

- For vegans, salad should comprise of greens, vegetables and fruits.

12) Name few vegetables that are commonly used in salad preparation.

Cucumber, Carrot, Potatoes, Artichokes, Broccoli, Cabbage, Cauliflower etc.

13) What are Classic salads?

Traditional salads that have gained popularity over years because of its unique combinations, great taste and flavour are known as Classic salads. Today, these salads have many variations.

14) Give few examples for Classic salads.

Ambrosia, Caesar salad, Cobb salad and Salade Niçoise.

15) What is a Candle salad?

It's a classic salad, believed to have been evolved in 1920s with ingredients such as pineapple, banana, cherry, green pepper with mayonnaise dressing.

16) Name the salad which is named after a hotel located in the New York City.

Waldorf salad (Waldorf Astoria Hotel).

17) Name the creator of Waldorf salad.

Oscar Michel Tschirky, a maître d'hôtel who was working in Waldorf Astoria Hotel.

18) Mention the ingredients used in Waldorf salad.

Apple, celery, grapes and walnut served on a bed of lettuce. The dressing consists of mayonnaise and lemon juice. Salt and pepper are added to adjust the taste.

19) Name the inventor of Caesar salad

Caesar Cardini invented the salad in the year 1924 at his Italian restaurant which was located in Tijuana, Mexico.

20) Name the fish used in Caesar salad.

Anchovies.

21) Give the components of Caesar salad.

Anchovies, coddled eggs, croutons, garlic flavoured oil, lemon juice, Parmesan cheese, Romaine lettuce and Worcestershire sauce. Salt and pepper are added to adjust the taste.

22) What is Olivier salad popularly known as?

Russian salad/Salade russe.

23) Name the Chef who introduced Russian salad.

Chef Lucien Olivier.

24) What are the ingredients used in Russian salad?

Cooked vegetables (potatoes, carrot, green peas) cut into dices, cooked meat and fish in dices, fresh cucumber, olives, salt, pepper and mayonnaise dressing.

25) What are the different garnishes of Russian salad?

Capers, gherkins, hard boiled eggs, fillets of anchovies, ox's tongue, truffles etc.

26) Name the Chef who is linked with the origin of Chef/Chef's salad

Chef Louis Diat of Ritz-Carlton, New York.

27) Name the salad which is sometimes referred as 'King of Salads'

Crab Louie/Louis Salad.

28) Which salad was born in the year 1937 when the Restaurant Manager of The Brown Derby, Los Angeles found a way to get rid of the left overs?

Cobb Salad.

29) Give one easy way to remember the ingredients used in making Cobb salad

Expand the words-EAT COBB.E-egg, A-avocado, T-tomato, C-chicken, O-onion, B-bacon and B-blue cheese.

30) What is Garden salad popularly known as?

Green salad.

31) Give two examples for rice based salads.

Maharajah salad and Oriental salad.

32) Name 7 international salads with its country of origin

Salad	*Country of origin*
Caesar	Mexico
Coleslaw	Netherlands
Crab Louie/Louis	United States
Greek	Greece
Niçoise	France
Russian	Russia
Waldorf	United States

33) Name few pasta (farinaceous) salads

Macaroni salad, Greek Pasta salad and Penne Pasta salad.

34) Name two bread salads

Fattoush (Lebanon) and Panzanella (Tuscany).

35) Name few fish salads

Tuna salad, Niçoise salad and Dutch Herring salad.

36) Name the kitchen equipment used to remove excess water from the salad greens.

Salad tosser/Salad spinner.

37) Name the salad created to resemble the three colours of Italian flag.

Caprese salad.

38) What is a dressing?

Dressing is an important component of a salad which is either loosened or thickened liquid with seasonings and flavourings. The role of a dressing is to increase the taste, appearance and palatability of a salad. Few of the dressings could be used as dips as well.

39) Which are the two main types of salad dressings?

Vinaigrette and Mayonnaise dressings.

40) Name few types of vinegar used in salad dressing.

Balsamic vinegar, Cider vinegar (Mild flavour with sweetness), Sherry vinegar, Red wine vinegar (highly acidic with red wine as its base) etc.

41) Name few kinds of juices used in salad dressing

Lemon juice, Lime juice and Verjuice.

42) Give examples for salad dressing.

French dressing, English dressing, acidulated cream dressing, mayonnaise dressing etc.

43) How will you make French dressing?

Combine 1 teaspoon of French mustard with a pinch of cayenne pepper, salt, pepper, caster sugar, 6 teaspoons of olive oil and 1 teaspoon of vinegar.(Oil:Vinegar-6:1)

44) How English dressing is made?

Mix 1 teaspoon of English mustard with a pinch of cayenne pepper, salt, pepper, caster sugar, 1 teaspoon of olive oil and 2 teaspoons of vinegar.(Oil:Vinegar-1:2)

45) What are the ingredients of acidulated cream dressing?

Lemon juice, salt, single cream and paprika.

46) How a simple lemon dressing is prepared?

It is made by combining oil, lemon juice and salt.

47) What is vinaigrette dressing?

Vinaigrette dressing is a cold dressing used in salads by mixing oil, vinegar, French and English mustard, salt and pepper.

48) Give few variations of Vinaigrette dressing

Tomato Vinaigrette, Lemon Vinaigrette, Honey Vinaigrette, Garlic Vinaigrette, Herb Vinaigrette etc.

49) What is Yogurt dressing?

Yogurt + Lemon juice + Dijon style mustard + Salt + Black pepper + Honey.

50) What is Thousand Island dressing?

Red & Green Pimento + Eggs + Parsley + Tabasco sauce + Vinegar + Oil + Salt + Pepper.

51) What is Oriental dressing?

Sunflower oil + Dark Soy sauce + Dry Sherry + Chinese Five spice powder + Garlic Clove + Honey.

52) Give an example for Cheese dressing

Roquefort dressing (Roquefort cheese+French dressing)

53) Name the first painter to introduce salad in his paintings

Leonardo da Vinci.

54) Name the salad named after City of Capri in Italy

Caprese salad.

55) A salad in a café in Bandra, Mumbai is named after a famous bollywood actress. Who is the celebrity?

Jacqueline Fernandez

56) Name the most popular salad dressing in U.S

Ranch dressing.

57) What is a Salad bar?

Salad bar is a counter that provides different ingredients to a guest for making his own salad.

58) Name the process responsible for turning few fruits to brown colour when exposed to air.

Oxidation.

59) What are the ingredients of Greek salad?

Cucumber, Onion, Tomato, Olives, Feta cheese, Oregano and Salt with Olive oil dressing.

60) What are the ingredients of Chef salad?

Hard-boiled eggs, Tomatoes, Cheese, Cucumber, Varieties of meat with French dressing.

61) What are the ingredients of Coleslaw?

Raw cabbage finely shredded with vinaigrette dressing.

62) Name the first book that was exclusively written for popularizing salads

The book titled 'Salads and Salad Making' which was published in the year 1883.

63) What is Salmagundi?

Salmagundi refers to a mixed salad that comprises of anchovies, chopped meat, eggs and vegetables with a dressing.

64) What are salad greens?

Salad green refers to the leaves of vegetables used in the preparation of salads.

65) Give two examples for salad greens.

Lettuce and chicory.

66) What is Lettuce?

Lettuce is a leafy green vegetable that belongs to the sunflower family which is used primarily in salads.

67) What is the scientific name of Lettuce?

Lactuca sativa, lactuca means 'milk forming' and sativa means 'common'.

68) What are the different types of lettuce?

Iceberg (Crisphead), Romaine (Cos), Butterhead, Looseleaf etc.

69) Where was lettuce first cultivated?

Lettuce is believed to have been first cultivated in ancient Egypt.

70) How Iceberg lettuce got its name?

It got its name due to the way it was packed and transported in trains. It was placed on top of crushed ice and transported from one place to another.

71) Why Romaine lettuce is also called as Cos lettuce?

The reason being Romaine lettuce first originated in Cos, Greece.

72) What are the uses of lettuce?

It could be used as a base for variety of salads. It's also used as an ingredient in soups and sandwiches.

73) Commercially, which lettuce is more important?

Iceberg lettuce is of utmost importance followed by Romaine lettuce.

74) What is Radicchio?

Radicchio is a type of chicory with deep purple-reddish leaves used in various salads.

75) What kind of salad is Fruit salad?

A type of salad made with fruits and can be served as dessert.

4.7 Sauce

1) What is a Sauce?

Sauce is a liquid or semi-liquid mixture which enhances the taste of a food item.

2) What are the characteristics of a good sauce?

A good sauce is smooth and light. It will compliment a dish, improves the texture and flavor at the same time never overpowers the taste of the food.

3) Name few roles played by sauces in the culinary world.

It is mostly served as an accompaniment of a main dish, gives moistness to the food, aids in digestion and increases the nutritive value of the food.

4) Name few ingredients required to make sauce.

Stock, Oil, Butter, Cream, Egg, Herbs, Condiments etc.

5) Name the chef who is responsible for preparing sauces in a kitchen.

Saucier.

6) Who was the first to categorize sauces?

Marie Antoine-Carême, a French chef.

7) Name the sauces categorized by the French chef, Marie Antoine-Carême as base sauces.

Béchamel sauce, Espagnole sauce, Velouté sauce and Allemande sauce.

8) What is a mother sauce/grand sauce?

The term refers to a sauce which serves as the base for making other sauces.

9) Why few sauces are called as mother sauces?

Since these sauces are the base for making many other sauces they are often called as mother sauces.

10) How many mother sauces are there?

Six.

11) Which are the different mother sauces?

Mayonnaise sauce, Béchamel sauce, Espagnole sauce, Velouté sauce, Hollandaise sauce and Tomato sauce.

12) What are emulsion sauces?

Emulsion sauces are those sauces made with ingredients which won't mix together easily. Such sauces become unstable if kept too long.

13) Give three examples for emulsion sauces.

Mayonnaise sauce, Hollandaise sauce and Vinaigrette.

14) Give two examples for egg based emulsion sauces.

Mayonnaise sauce and Hollandaise sauce.

15) Name the sauce which is popularly referred as 'White sauce'.

Béchamel sauce.

16) Which sauce is known as Brown sauce?

Espagnole.

17) Which sauce is popularly referred as 'Cold sauce'?

Mayonnaise sauce.

18) Name the ingredients used to prepare Mayonnaise sauce.

Egg yolk, salad oil, mustard and seasonings.

19) Name few derivatives of Mayonnaise sauce.

Tartare sauce, Thousand Island dressing and Cocktail sauce.

20) What is Roux?

An equal quantity of flour and butter cooked together is known as Roux.

21) Give any two functions of Roux.

- ➢ Roux could be used as a thickening agent in sauces and soups.
- ➢ When added, it improves the flavor of the preparation.

22) Which are the three kinds of Roux?

White roux, Blond roux and Brown roux.

23) Give the time required to make different kinds of Roux.

Type of roux	Time required
White roux	3 to 5 minutes
Blond roux	5 to 10 minutes
Brown roux	15 to 20 minutes

24) Which are the ingredients used to make Béchamel sauce?

Roux, Milk and Bouquet garni.

25) Mention the French courtier after whom Béchamel sauce is named.

Louis de Béchamel.

26) Name few derivatives of Béchamel sauce.

Mornay sauce, Cardinal sauce and Soubise sauce.

27) Give four derivatives of Espagnole sauce.

Demi glace, Diable sauce, Madeira sauce and Vin rouge sauce.

28) Which are the derivatives of Velouté sauce?

Allemande sauce, Bercy sauce, Normande sauce, Supreme sauce etc.

29) Give two derivatives of Hollandaise sauce.

Mousseline sauce and Maltaise sauce.

30) Name three derivatives of Tomato sauce.

Creole sauce, Portugaise sauce and Milanaise sauce.

31) What is the difference between a gravy and sauce?

Gravy is prepared from the juices of meat by adding seasonings and generally without any thickening agents. On the other hand, sauces are prepared with thickeners by adding it to liquid seasoning.

32) What are derivative sauces?

Derivative sauces are sauces that are derived from basic mother sauces.

33) Which are the four parts of a sauce?

A sauce generally consists of four parts namely liquid, thickening agents, flavouring agents and seasonings.

34) There is always a risk of curdling of mayonnaise sauce. Give any two reasons.

> If fresh egg yolks are not used in preparation

> The vessel and equipment used for the preparation is unclean.

35) Give two examples for dessert (sweet) sauces.

Caramel sauce and Cherry sauce.

4.8 Soup

1) What is Soup?

Soup is a healthy, nutritious food in the liquid or semi-liquid form made either from meat or vegetable stock.

2) What makes soup a healthy food?

Soups are generally low in calories and have perfect balance between carbohydrates, proteins, fats, vitamins and minerals.

3) What is the base/foundation of soup?

Stock.

4) What is stock?

Stock is a liquid flavoured with different ingredients used as a base for soups and stews.

5) Which are the three most important stocks?

White stock (made from white meat), Brown stock (made using beef and veal) and Vegetable stock (made from vegetables and herbs).

6) Which are the Italian and German terms for soup?

Zuppa/La Minestra (Italian) and Suppe (German).

7) Under which course 'soup' is served in French classical menu?

Soup is generally served under course no. 2, Potage.

8) What does the word 'Potage' mean?

The word 'Potage' in French generally refers to thick soup and it means 'cooked in a pot'.

9) What is the origin of the word 'soup'?

The word soup is derived from the Latin word, 'suppa'.

10) What are the characteristics of a 'good' soup?

A good soup

- Should feature fresh, locally available ingredients
- Should have enticing aroma
- Should have restorative properties.

11) Name few garnishes used in soup

Croutons, grated cheese, sour cream, pasta, meat, seafood, vegetables, rice etc.

12) Name few accompaniments offered along with soup

Melba toast, Bread rolls, Bread sticks, Baguette, Cheese straws, Corn chips, Crackers etc.

13) Which is the oldest known soup?

Lentil soup as per Bible.

14) According to the archeological evidence, which is the oldest soup?

Hippopotamus soup.

15) Which is the costliest soup in the world? (As per Guinness Book of World Records)

'Buddha jumps over the wall', a soup made with the fin of shark, sea cucumber, chicken, ham, dried scallops, pork etc. available for $190 at Kai Mayfair Restaurant, London is the costliest soup in the world.

16) What are the different types of soups?

Thick, thin, cold, national & international soups.

17) What are thin soups?

Thin soups are soups that are clear, unthickened and clarified.

18) How thin soups are classified?

Thin soups are classified as passed and unpassed soups.

19) What is the cover for thin soup?

Thin soup is served in a soup bowl along with its saucer and soup spoon.

20) What is a Passed (Clear) soup?

Passed soup is a soup which is strained after its preparation. As a result the soup is clear without any solid ingredients. Consommé is an example for the same.

21) What is Consommé?

Consommé refers to clarified and flavoured beef stock.

22) What do you mean by 'clarifying' a Consommé?

Clarifying refers to the use of egg whites and lean meat for removing fat and other sediments present in the soup.

What makes the clarification of Consommé possible?

The coagulation of egg whites and lean meat makes the clarification of Consommé possible.

23) What does the word 'Consommé' mean?

According to the website spruceeats.com, the word Consommé means 'completed' or 'concentrated' in French.

24) Give four examples for Consommé

Consommé Carmen, Consommé Julienne, Consommé Andalouse and Consommé Royale.

25) Is it true that Consommés are named after its garnish?

Yes, Consommés are generally named after its garnish.

26) How consommés are served in restaurants?

Consommés are served in a consommé cup along with the saucer. A sweet spoon is also placed as part of the cover.

27) Why a sweet spoon is placed as part of the cover when consommés are served?

The guest is expected to use a sweet spoon for consuming the garnish of the consommé offered.

28) What is Jellied Consommé?

Jellied Consommé is a type of consommé which is thickened using the gelatin obtained from animal bones. It has jelly like consistency and is served cold.

29) Give an example for Jellied Consommé.

Jellied Consommé Madrilène.

30) What are unpassed soups?

Unpassed soups are those soups that are not strained and features solid ingredients. Examples include Bouillons and Broths.

31) What are Broths?

Thin soups that are not clarified are referred to as Broths.

32) What is the difference between broth and stock?

Broth is made by simmering vegetables and meat whereas bones and vegetables are simmered for making stock.

33) What is Bouillon?

Bouillon is unclarified broth made from meat or vegetables.

34) What is the main difference between a 'passed' and 'unpassed' soup?

A passed soup is strained where as an unpassed one is not strained.

35) What are thick soups?

Thick soups are soups that are thick in nature. The thickness is obtained by the addition of thickening agents in various forms.

36) Name one thickening agent used in thick soups.

Roux.

37) What is the cover for thick soup?

Soup plate, underliner and soup spoon.

38) Classify thick soups.

Bisque, Chowder, Cream, Purée and Velouté.

39) What is Bisque?

Bisque is a shellfish based soup finished with cream. For imparting flavour, either wine or brandy is added.

40) Name the traditional thickening agent used in bisque.

Rice (starch).

41) What is Chowder?

A seafood based American soup.

42) How is Chowder thickened?

Chowder soup is thickened using any of the given ingredients-Roux and Broken crackers.

43) What is a 'Crème' soup?

'Crème' means Cream and is a purée soup, thickened with béchamel sauce and finished with either milk or cream. Cream soups generally get its name from the main ingredient used in its making.

44) What do you mean by the term 'Purée'?

Purée is a category of soups made from the purée of the main ingredient used in the soup. It could also feature milk or cream but is not as smooth as cream soups.

45) What is Velouté soup?

Velouté soup is a kind of soup thickened with blond roux or veloute sauce, egg yolk, butter and cream.

46) What are Fruit soups?

These soups could be served either cold or warm and has a fruit as its main ingredient. Sour cherry soup and Coconut soup are examples.

47) What is Cold Soup?

Soups that are served cold are termed as Cold Soups.

48) What is Gazpacho?

A tomato and vegetable based soup from Spain which is served cold.

49) What are canned soups?

These are 'ready-to-eat' soups prepared with the addition of water for any time use.

50) What are Condensed soups?

These are soups from which much of the water is eliminated. Before serving, it is heated with either water or milk.

51) What was Alphabet soup?

Alphabet soup was a type of condensed soup popular in US that featured pasta in the shape of alphabets.

52) What are Pocket soups?

Pocket soup or Portable soup was a type of dehydrated food and was similar to bouillon cubes. The convenience to carry and its shelf life made it quite popular.

53) What is Gumbo?

Gumbo is a very strong, flavourful soup that comes from the U.S state of Louisiana.

54) Name the soup in which dried Sassafras leaves are used as flavouring and thickening agent.

Gumbo.

55) Name the soup from Louisiana which is traditionally served over rice.

Gumbo.

56) Are all soups served hot?

No, few soups such as Gazpacho and Fruit soup are served cold.

57) What is Bird's Nest Soup?

Bird's Nest Soup, a delicacy in Chinese cuisine is an expensive soup made using bird's nest and other ingredients. The nest is the saliva of the bird in dried and hardened form. It claims to have medicinal properties too.

58) As per tradition, which bird's nest is used to make Bird's Nest Soup?

Swiftlet bird's nest is used.

59) Name the soup popular as 'Gratinée Lyonnaise' in France

French Onion Soup.

60) Name the traditional cheese used in French Onion Soup.

Gruyere cheese.

61) Name the traditional fish used in making Bouillabaisse.

Rascasse.

62) Which is the birthplace of Bouillabaisse?

Old Port of Marseille, France.

63) Name three soups with wine as an ingredient

Consommé au vin (Madeira/Port wine) and Consommé chasseur (Madeira) and Soupe de tortue au Xérès (Sherry).

64) Name a soup which is ideal to serve during the Christmas season

Soupe aux cerises (Cherry soup).

65) What is the Japanese equivalent of Consommé?

Dashi.

66) Give two examples for heavy soups.

Minestrone and Seafood chowder.

67) What is Borsch/Borscht?

Borsch is a Russian/Ukranian beet soup with vegetables and served with sour cream.

68) Name two soups which could be consumed either warm or cold.

Borsch and Vichyssoise.

69) Name two stew like soups.

Garbure (France) and Minestrone (Italy).

70) Name the French soup which is served in the pot in which it is cooked.

Petite Marmite.

71) Which soup literally means 'little pot'?

Petite Marmite.

72) What is Shorba?

Shorba, the word comes from the Arab word, 'Shurbah' and refers to a type of flavourful, thin soup.

73) Give two examples for Shorba.

Tamatar ka Shorba and Kashmiri Yakhni Shorba.

74) What are regional soups?

These are soups that come from a particular area.

75) What is imitation shark fin soup?

This soup is an imitation of the famous shark fin soup. It is made with noodles and other gelatinous products.

76) What is Oxtail soup?

Oxtail is a kind of soup made with oxtail and vegetables.

77) Which Italian soup literally means 'that which is served'?

Minestrone.

78) Name the split pea soup from Netherlands which is served with rye bread.

Snert.

79) Which Scottish soup is traditionally garnished with juliennes of prunes?

Cock-a-leekie.

80) What is the meaning of the word 'Mulligatawny'?

Pepper water.

81) Mention the national soup of Thailand.

Tom Yum.

82) Give two examples for each category of soups.

Soup	Examples
Bisque	Lobster bisque and Shrimp bisque
Bouillon	Bouillon aux herbes and Bouillon de légumes
Broth	Chicken broth and Vegetable broth
Cold soup	Borscht and Gazpacho
Consommé	Consommé Brunoise and Consommé Indienne
Chowder	Clam chowder and Corn chowder
Cream soup	Cream of Celery and Cream of Chicken
International soup	Borscht and Minestrone
Purée soup	Potage Purée de Céleri and Potage Purée de Marrons
Velouté soup	Velouté de volaille and Velouté d'asperge

83) Give the names of international soups with its country of origin

Name of the soup	Country of origin
Albondigas soup *(Meatballs soup with tortilla)*	Mexico
Avgolemono *(Chicken soup with lemon and egg)* Fasolada *(Bean soup)*	Greece
Borscht *(Beetroot and vegetable soup)*	Russia
Caldo Verde *(Green soup)*	Portugal

Continued…

Cock-a-leekie soup	Scotland
(Leek and potato soup)	
French Onion soup	France
(Caramelised onion soup)	
Gazpacho	Spain
(Cold tomato soup)	
Green turtle soup	England
(Consommé with turtle meat)	
Gumbo	US
(Meat soup with okra)	
Kohl Suppe	Austria
(Cabbage soup)	
Minestrone soup	Italy
(Pasta soup)	
Miso soup	Japan
(Seaweed soup)	
Mulligatawny soup	India
(Curried lentil soup)	
Shark Fin Soup	China
(Shark fin in broth)	

84) Do we drink or eat soup?

According to exports, we eat soup.

85) What are Dessert soups?

Soups that are sweet in taste and consumed as part of the dessert course are termed as Dessert soups.

86) Give few examples for Dessert soups.

Kissel (Russia) and Mango Pomelo Sago (China).

87) Name the thickening agents used in gumbo.

Filé, Okra and Roux.

88) What is Gründonnerstagsuppe?

It's a green coloured soup that consists of 7 to 9 green herbs, traditionally served in Germany on Maundy Thursday.

89) Name a soup which is prepared with coconut milk.

Tom Kha Gai soup from Thailand.

90) Why soups are generally served as starters?

Drinking soup in the beginning of a meal aids in the secretion of digestive juices in the digestive tract.

CHAPTER-5

Beverages

Section no.	Sub-heading	Questions
5.1	Beer	128
5.2	Cocktails	135
5.3	Mocktails	25
5.4	Liqueurs	130
5.5	Liquors	406
5.6	Tea, Coffee & Energy drinks	80
5.7	Water	40
5.8	Wine	265

5.1 Beer

1) What is Beer?

Beer is a brewed alcoholic beverage made from malted barley.

2) Give one difference between beer and wine.

Beer is made from grains whereas wine is produced from fruits.

3) Which is the Latin word from which the term 'beer' originated?

The word 'beer' originated from the Latin word 'biber'

4) Name few grains used to make beer other than barley.

Wheat, rice, maize, corn, sorghum, millet etc.

5) Give the names of few beer gods and goddesses of ancient times.

Gods-Sucellus and Radegast.

Goddesses-Ninkasi, Nephthys and Tenenet.

6) Name the praising hymn written by the Sumerians for their beer goddess.

'The Sumerian Hymn to Ninkasi.'

7) Who was Ninkasi?

Ninkasi was the Sumerian goddess of beer and brewing.

8) Name the birth place of modern beer.

Babylon (ancient Babylonia).

9) Name the four basic ingredients used in beer making.

Water, Barley, Hops and Yeast.

10) Name the widely used flavouring agent in beer.

Hops.

11) What is Hops?

A hop is a type of flower that belongs to the Humulus lupulus family.

12) Name the predecessor of hops.

Gruit.

13) Who were the first to add hops to beer?

Monks were the first to add hops to the beer.

14) Give the role of hops in beer.

Hops impart bitterness, floral and herbal aromas to the beer. It balances the sweetness of malt, acts as a preservative and has natural antiseptic qualities.

15) Name the compound present in hops that imparts bitter flavor.

Lupulin.

16) Name few well known hops used in making beer.

Name	Aroma	Country of origin
Cascade	Citrus	US
Chinook	Citrus	US
Fuggles	Floral	US & UK
Tettang	Spicy	Germany
Willamette	Spicy, floral & fruity	US

17) Give the unit of measurement of Hops bitterness level in beer.

International Bitter Units (IBU).

18) Name few alternatives to hops.

Mugwort (aromatic plant), heather (perennial shrub), chamomile tea etc.

19) Name the process by which beer is made.

Brewing.

20) Who were the first to record the brewing process?

Egyptians were the first to record the brewing process.

21) Which process in beer making converts starch into sugar?

Malting.

22) What does the term 'malted' mean in malted barley?

The term 'malted' is used to refer the grains that have undergone germination and then dried. Malting helps in developing the enzymes or proteins that generate chemical reactions which are needed to turn the starch into sugar.

23) Why barely is widely preferred by the brewers to make beer?

Barley's fibrous husk (aids in brewing) and high concentration of amylase (an enzyme that converts starch to sugar) makes it superior than other grains (rye, wheat, oats etc.).

24) Name the variety of barley used in beer making.

Hordeum sativum.

25) Name few clarifying agents used in beer.

Isinglass (bladder of sturgeon fish), Irish moss (from red algae), Kappa carrageenan (from sea weed) and Gelatin

26) What is Brewer's Yeast?

Each brewer develops a specific yeast strain belonging to Saccharomyces species which is known as Brewer's Yeast. Examples are ale yeast (saccharomyces cerevisiae) and lager yeast (saccharomyces carlsbergensis).

27) What is the role of yeast in beer making?

Yeast is responsible for the fermentation process, contributes to the fruitiness and other flavour characteristics of beer.

28) What are 'adjuncts' in beer making?

Adjuncts is a term used to denote different cereals like rice and corn which is added to barley just before malting for improving the flavour and colour of beer.

29) What are 'additives' in beer making?

Additives are chemicals that are added to the beer to impart certain qualities. Example-Gum Arabic is added to the beer to stabilise the froth.

30) What do you mean by 'malting' in the process of making beer?

Malting is the germination and subsequent drying of the barley.

31) Name the enzyme produced due to sprouting of barley.

Amylase/Diastase.

32) What is green malt?

The germinated and sprouted barley is referred to as green malt.

33) What is Peat?

Peat is a dark, blackish coloured acidic fuel made from decaying plant matter. It is used while drying barley and it provides earthy fragrance to it.

34) What is Peat's reek?

The pungent, earthy fragrance which the barley develops during the drying process in a kiln is termed as Peat's reek.

35) What is Kilning?

The process of drying barley in hot air (which happens in a kiln) is called Kilning.

36) What is milling?

The process of grinding malted barley using grinders is milling.

37) What is Grist?

Milled or powdered malt is termed as Grist.

38) What is Mash tun?

Mash tun is a large vessel made of stainless steel or cast iron with mechanical stirrers and has a base of perforated steel. Grist along with hot water is churned violently in a mash tun.

39) What is Wort?

When grist along with hot water is churned in a mash tun the resultant product is a sweetish liquid called Wort.

40) What is Lautering?

Lautering is the step carried out to segregate mash from wort.

41) What is Lauter Tun?

Lauter tun is a kind of vessel with filters used to segregate mash from wort

42) What is Sparging?

The process of trickling water on the mash to extract more sugar is termed as Sparging.

43) What is Hopping?

The process of adding hops to wort is termed as Hopping.

44) What is brewing?

Brewing is a process of boiling, wort, hops and sugar in a brew kettle.

45) What is brew kettle?

A large copper kettle used to boil wort, hops and sugar.

46) What is Pitching?

The process of adding yeast to the wort is known as Pitching.

47) What is top fermentation process?

Top fermentation process of beer is carried out by using top cropping yeasts called as Saccharomyces cervisiae. The temperature varies from 15-25°C. It takes almost 3 to 7 days for proper fermentation. Ale beer follows this method.

48) What is bottom fermentation process?

Bottom fermentation requires lower temperature, 5-10°C and the fermentation process is activated by bottom cropping yeasts known as Saccharomyces carlsbergensis. It takes almost 2 weeks for proper fermentation. After this the yeast starts settling in the bottom of the vat. Lager beer is prepared in this fashion.

49) What is pasteurization of beer?

Pasteurization of beer refers to the process of heating beer at 60-66°C for nearly 20 minutes-1 hour by passing it through a tube or through a heated tunnel. This step prevents the microbial growth in it and increases the shelf life of beer

50) Why keg (draught) beer taste better than canned or bottled beer?

Pasteurization involves heating which removes the taste of beer. Keg beer is not exposed to this process and hence it tastes better than canned or bottled beer.

51) How beer can be stored?

It can be stored in kegs, casks, cans and bottles.

52) Which are the main types of beer?

The main types of beer are ale, lager and speciality beers.

53) What is Ale beer?

Ale beer is the world's oldest beer and the term 'ale' covers almost all the top fermented beers that are made in British style. All ale beers are full bodied and fruity. The colour mostly is amber and the flavour can be bitter, sweet and sour.

54) What are the different types of ale beer?

Stout, Porter, Wheat, Barley wine etc.

55) What is Stout beer?

Stout beer is a top fermented beer that posses deep black colour with the flavour of toasted malt. It is firm with creamy forth and can be sweet, bitter or dry. Sometimes caramel sugar is added to it for colour and taste. Hop content is high in this beer. Stout beer is sold in bottles and served in room temperature. The various types of stout beer include Dry stout, Imperial stout, Oatmeal stout etc.

56) What is Porter beer?

Porter beer is a type of ale beer which is full flavoured and highly aromatic. It is a dark beer that is brewed from charred malt. The porters at London's Victoria station used to mix several styles of beer together for consumption. Thus Porter beer was born. The first brewer that offered this beer commercially was Arthur Guinness and Sons.

57) What is Wheat beer?

A type of top fermented beer made primarily from wheat with the addition of barley. Weizebier/Weissbier is a popular variety of wheat beer from Bavaria, Germany. This cloudy ale beer is made from special strains of yeasts which finally imparts the taste of cloves and banana to the beer.

58) What is Barley wine?

This beer has alcohol content equal to most of the wines. The colour varies from straw to dark. The aroma of malt, hops and alcohol can be felt. This beer can be stored for a longer duration because of the preserving qualities of alcohol. Barley wine is strongest of all other British ale styles.

59) What is Lager beer?

Lager beer is believed to have been invented by Bavarian monks and is the most consumed beer in the world. Lager is a term applied to beers made by bottom fermentation method. The word 'lager' comes from the German term called 'lagern' which means 'to store'. The fermentation process is slower in comparison to ale and is carried out at very low temperatures (5-10°C). The heavier yeasts (Saccharomyces carlsbergensis/uvarum) settle down after fermentation. This type of beer has thinner body and is often dryMost Australian and European beers that are available are lagers. Notable lager beers are Pilsner, Bock, Märzen etc.

60) What is Pilsner/Pils/Pilsener beer?

This lager beer comes from the Czech town of Plzen and is the world's most popular style of beer. The alcohol content of this beer varies from 4.5-5.5%. This beer has moderate hop bitterness and light maltiness. As per the actual recipe it is full bodied, but nowadays it is thin and neutral.

61) What is Bock beer?

Bock comes from Einbeck, a German village. This beer has high alcohol content (more than 6%) and has malty sweetness. Bock is matured for a longer period of time and is a seasonal beer. Bock means 'billy goat' and a goat's head can be viewed on the beer label. Doppelbock is a variation of Bock.

62) What is Ice beer?

Ice beer is a type of pale lager beer with high alcoholic content. The beer is frozen right after the brewing process, thereby enabling the water present in the beer to be frozen up. The water that has become ice crystals will be finally removed, resulting in the increase of alcohol content of the beer. This kind of beer is not that expensive.

63) What is Märzen beer?

A German beer brewed in the month of March is Märzen beer. It has got malty aroma and has alcoholic content more than 5.5%.The colour varies from pale to dark brown and style from medium to full body. This Bavarian beer is served during Oktoberfest.

64) Differentiate ale from lager beer.

Criteria of differentiation	*Ale*	*Lager*
Type of yeast used	Saccharomyces cervisiae	Saccharomyces carlsbergensis/uvarum
Fermentation temperature	Warmer temperature (15-25°C)	Cooler temperature (5-10°C)
Fermentation process	Made by top fermentation method	Made by bottom fermentation method
Fermentation period	Fermentation period is shorter than lager beer (takes few days)	Fermentation period is longer than ale beer (takes weeks/months)
Taste	Stronger in taste than lager	Less stronger in taste
Serving temperature	Ales are best served at 10-13°C	Lagers are best served at 4-7°C
Examples	Ales include Stouts, Porters, Pale Ales, Wheat Ales etc.	Lagers include Pilsners, Helles, Bocks etc.

64) What is speciality beer?

Speciality beer could be either ale or lager to which flavours are added.

65) What is Fruit beer?

Fruit beer could be either ale or lager and is flavoured with different types of fruits. Lakefront Cherry Lager and Marin Blueberry Flavoured Ale from United States are good examples.

66) What is Vegetable beer?

Vegetable flavoured ale or lager beer. Brooklyn's Post Road Pumpkin Ale from USA is a good example for the same.

67) What is Weizenbier?

This Bavarian beer, also known as Weissbier is a cloudy ale made from malted wheat and barley. Special strains of yeasts are used which finally imparts the taste of cloves and banana to the beer. This beer is best taken with a twist of lemon.

68) What is Smoked beer?

Smoked beer, also known as Rauchbier predominantly comes from Bamberg, Germany. It posses smoky flavour and is made by drying malt over smoking wood or peat. Smoked beer can be either top fermented or bottom fermented.

69) What is Lambic (Lambiek) beer?

Lambic beer is a kind of sour beer hailing from Brussels, capital of Belgium. It is made by spontaneous fermentation and is matured in oak barrels for a longer period of time. Aged hops are added to the cool wort which is exposed to bacteria forming a sour beer which is later on sweetened and blended with low alcohol content.

70) What is Draught/Draft/Tap beer?

Draught beer is a type of beer mostly served in pubs and bars. It comes in keg or barrel from the brewery and is connected to a machine for the service purpose. When the beer tap is opened, beer flows from the keg through a pipe and is infused with carbon dioxide gas. The beer is normally un-pasteurised and could be either ale or lager.

71) What is the difference between LABs and NABs?

LAB stands for Low Alcoholic Beers and refers to beer with 1.2% alcoholic content by volume. NAB stands for Non- Alcoholic Beers and refers to beer with 0.5% alcoholic content by volume.

72) What do you mean by the term 'Craft beer'?

It's a term that is still on debate. But according to The Brewer's Association in Boulder, Colorado, Craft beer is a beer made by a brewer that is small, independent and traditional.

73) What is a Trappist Beer?

Beer produced and sold under the strict guidelines of The International Trappist Association (ITA) is termed as Trappist Beer.

74) What is unusual about Kelpie Beer?

Kelpie Beer is a seaweed beer without hops manufactured by Heather Ale in Strathaven, Scotland. It is a type of ale beer with dark brown colour that possesses 4.4% ABV.

75) What is brewery or brew house?

Brewery or brew house refers to a place where beer is brewed.

76) What is microbrewery?

Microbrewery is a type of brewery that produces very limited no. of beer every year such as less than 15,000 barrels of beer every year.

77) What is macro brewery?

A micro brewery is a brewery that produces beer in large quantities.

78) Name the oldest operating brewery in the world.

Weihenstephan, Germany.

79) Give the term used to denote a woman who brews beer.

Brewster.

80) Name the beer brand with the highest alcoholic content (as of April 2021).

Snake Venom by Brewmeister Brewery, Scotland with an alcoholic content of 67.5%.

81) Which beer brand features orange slice as its garnish.

Blue Moon.

82) Give an example for a sour beer.

Geuze.

83) What is the study of beer and beer making called?

Zythology.

84) Name the largest beer festival in the world.

Oktoberfest. It is held at Munich, Bavaria, Germany.

85) Name the Belgian beer brand which was banned in U.S as its label featured a naked little boy peeing.

Manneken Pis.

86) Where and when was Guinness brewery born?

Guinness brewery was opened in 1759 at Dublin, Ireland.

87) Name the largest brewer of stout beer in the world.

Guinness Brewery/St.James's Gate Brewery, Ireland.

88) What is the actual colour of Guinness Porter beer?

It might appear black though it's actually a dark shade of ruby.

89) What is the logo of Guinness beer brand?

It's a harp with its straight edge facing the left side.

90) Name the round, plastic sphere seen in a can of Guinness beer.

Widget.

91) What is the purpose of 'widget' in can of Guinness beer?

The widget is a plastic, nitrogen-filled sphere that enables the carbon dioxide present in the beer to form a creamy head when the can is opened.

92) Which beer was born as a result of adding extra alcohol and hops to it on its voyage from Britain to India?

IPA.

93) What is IPA?

India Pale Ale is a style of beer with 5.5% to 7.5% alcohol content with good amount of hops in it. This beer was born in Britain and was intended to satisfy Britishers who were drinking this beer in Indian conditions.

94) What is a cask conditioned beer?

A beer served directly from the keg in which it was brewed is known as cask conditioned beer.

95) Name pizza flavoured beer.

'Mamma Mia! Pizza Beer' manufactured by Pizza Beer Company.

96) Which bird is seen in the logo of Costa Rican beer brand, Imperial?

Eagle.

97) Name the man who used hairs from his beard to create his own yeast for beer making.

John Maier of Rogue Ales, Oregon.

98) Give few health benefits of beer

➢ Improves bone density due to high levels of silicon in beer

> ➢ Aids in preventing blood clots and lowers one's cholesterol level

> ➢ Dark beer promotes digestion

99) Name the world's largest brewer.

Anheuser-Busch InBev.

100) Who is generally regarded as the patron saint of beer?

St. Arnold of Soissons.

101) What is the normal size of a beer can?

16 oz.

102) What is the standard size of Indian beer bottle?

650 ml.

103) What is Pint?

A term used to denote a 375 ml bottle.

104) Give international brand names of beer.

Aubel (Belgium), Carlsberg (Denmark), Corona Extra (Mexico), Quilmes (Argentina) and Snow (China).

105) Mention Indian brand names of beer.

Kingfisher, Royal Challenge, Haywards 5000, Knock out and King's.

106) Name four brands of beer from Japan.

Sapporo, Asahi, Kirin and Spring Valley.

107) Name four Chinese beer brands.

Tsing Tao, Peking, West Lake and Shanghai.

108) Which brewery produces largest number of Indian beer?

United Breweries based in Bangalore.

109) Which Indian beer has the tagline, 'The King of good times'?

Kingfisher.

110) Name India's first stout beer.

Simba Stout.

111) Which beer is traditionally served with wedge of lime?

Corona.

112) Which Cuban beer is named after an Indian chief?

Hatuey.

113) Which is the ancient Chinese beer made from wheat?

Samshu.

114) Name few beer glasses used in the service of beer.

Beer Tankard, Pilsner, Stange, Snifter, Thistle shaped beer glass etc.

115) How to serve beer?

- ➢ Lift the beer glassware and hold it by its base, at an angle of 45°

- ➢ Pour the beer slowly through the side of the glass encouraging head formation.

116) How to store beer?

- ➢ It's good to have a cellar with proper ventilation (located underground) for storing beer

- ➢ Beer bottles should be always stored upright

- ➢ Beer cans and bottles must be stored in cellar at a temperature of 13°C

- ➢ Beer stored in kegs must be stored cold till the time it is served.

117) Give some beer faults.

Smell in beer, Cloudy beer, Sour beer and Skunked beer.

118) When a beer bottle becomes 'skunked'?

When the beer bottles are exposed to light it becomes 'skunked'.

119) Which is the world's strongest beer?

Snake Venom made by Brewmeister Brewery, Scotland has 67.5 percent ABV.

120) Name the beer brand seen in the famous American cartoon, 'The Simpsons.'

Duff.

121) Which beer is named after the international telephone code of India?

Bira 91.

122) What does the term 'Light beer' printed on an American beer label and European beer label signify?

According to Americans, it refers to a beer that possesses 50% lesser calories than the traditional American beer. For Europeans, the term signifies a beer with light colour and body.

123) Name the national drink of Japan.

Sake.

124) Give the terms used to denote Sake.

Japanese rice beer or rice wine, Ninhonshu in Japanese.

125) How is Sake served?

Sake could be served either warm or cold.

126) Name few equipments used in the service of Sake.

Tokkuri (serving bottle), Sakazuki (small saucer like cup), Choko (small cup) and Masu (square cedar wood box).

127) What is sparkling Sake?

Sparkling Sake refers to sake with carbon dioxide in it. It generally has low alcoholic content and is sweet in taste. Suzune and Mio are brands.

128) Give few brand names of Sake.

Ozeki Nigori, Hakkaisan Ginjo, Kanchiku and Square One Junmai.

5.2 Cocktails

1) What is a Cocktail?

Cocktail is a term used to denote a drink made with one or more alcoholic beverages along with mixers such as fruit juices, aerated water etc. It's often served chilled.

2) Is Cocktail alcoholic?

Yes, Cocktail is alcoholic.

3) What are Classic cocktails?

According to Wikipedia, Classic cocktails are those cocktails which were printed in the book of bartender Jerry Thomas released in the year 1862 and published in the book of Harry Craddock in the year 1930.The cocktails that were born between 1862 and 1930 could also be referred as Classic Cocktails.

4) Name few classic cocktails

Gimlet *(1867)*, **Daiquiri** *(1896)*, **Dry Martini** *(1911)*, **Singapore Sling** *(1914)* and **Bloody Mary** *(1921)*.

5) What is a crafted cocktail?

Crafted cocktails feature fresh ingredients such as fresh fruits, fresh syrups and fresh juices in the cocktail. No preserved juices and ingredients are used in its making.

6) What is an IBA Cocktail?

IBA stands for International Bartenders Association and the term 'IBA cocktail' is used to denote cocktails which are mostly selected and prepared by bartenders for various international cocktail making competitions.

7) What is a 'Tiki' cocktail?

Tiki cocktail is a kind of cocktail that mostly features rum as its base with one or more fruit juices. They tend to have elaborated garnishes such as fruits, decorative straws and paper parasols. Few examples for Tiki cocktails are Mai Tai and Zombie.

8) What is DIY cocktail?

DIY cocktail means 'Do it Yourself'. These are cocktails that could be prepared at home or anywhere without the aid of bartenders. It comes as a kit and the user need to follow the instructions given and use the ingredients accordingly.

9) What are mixed drinks?

A mixed drink could be a mocktail or a cocktail and will feature more than one ingredient.

10) What are shooters?

A shooter is a type of drink served in shot glassware and is mostly consumed in one gulp. Examples include Bloody Mary shots and B-52.

11) Give two examples for flaming shooters.

Flaming Sambuca and flaming B-52.

12) What is B 50 series of layered shooters?

B 50 series of layered shooters refers to a number of layered shot cocktails from B-51 to B-57.

13) What is B-52?

A shooter made with Kahlúa, Grand Marnier and Bailey's Irish Cream.

14) What are barrel aged cocktails?

Barrel aged cocktails refer to those cocktails that are aged in wooden casks/barrels for few weeks. The bartender expects the cocktail to develop character and flavour like how wines and spirits do. Tony Conigliaro of 69 Colebrooke Row, London was the first who tried to age cocktails. He used glass containers for aging cocktails and later on another mixologist named Jeffrey Morgenthaler made use of barrels to age cocktails.

15) Name few cocktails that are good for barrel aging.

Old fashioned, Cosmopolitan, Vieux Carre, Manhattan, Sazerac etc.

16) What are Tropical Drinks?

Tropical drinks are those drinks which are served in decorative glasses with fancy or attractive garnishes. Most of the rum based cocktail falls under this category and is generally made by shaken or blending method. Fruit juices, syrups, coconut milk, cream and other flavours add charm to these drinks. Piña Colada, Planter's Punch, Zombie, Chi chi etc. are examples.

17) Name the different methods by which cocktails can be prepared.

Shaken method, Stirred method, Blend method and Build method.

18) Name few cocktails that are made by shaken method.

Piña Colada, White Lady, Bacardi Cocktail, Pink Lady, Daiquiri etc.

19) Name few cocktails that are prepared by stirred method.

Bloody Mary, Dry Martini, Manhattan etc.

20) Name two cocktails that are prepared by blending method.

Frozen Daiquiri and Daiquiri Mulata.

21) Name few cocktails that are prepared by build method.

Planter's Punch, Pousse Cafe, Tequila Sunrise, B 52 etc.

22) How many layers are there in a Pousse cafe cocktail?

The layer ranges from three (minimum) to seven (maximum).

23) What is frosting /rimming glassware?

It is the process of moistening the rim of a glassware using lemon juice, honey or any other form of syrups and placing it over sugar or salt to create an attractive rim. A glass rimmer makes this process easier.

24) What all liquid items can be used to rim a glass?

Lemon juice, Honey, Orange juice, Egg white, Sugar syrup, Grenadine syrup etc.

25) Name three cocktails that feature salted rim.

Bloody Mary, Margarita and Salty Dog.

26) Give the names of three cocktails that feature sugared rim.

Champagne Limoncello, Pink Lady **and** Side car.

27) What does the word 'Planters' in 'Planters Punch' cocktail refer to?

The word 'Planters' in 'Planters Punch' cocktail refers to the Planters Hotel located in Charleston, United States.

28) What does the word 'Ramos' in 'Ramos Gin Fizz' cocktail refer to?

The word 'Ramos' refers to the inventor of Ramos gin fizz cocktail, Henry C.Ramos.

29) Who/What is Don the beachcomber?

Don the beachcomber is the name of a bar and restaurant started by Donn Beach (Ernest Raymond).

30) Name the brandy based cocktail that features a long, thin lemon spiral rind as its garnish.

Horse's Neck.

31) Name a cocktail invented by a female bartender.

Hanky-Panky Cocktail.

32) Name few cocktails that can be served to ladies.

Pink Lady, Ladies Negroni and Sex on the beach.

33) Name few cocktails made with soda water.

Mojito, Gin Fizz, Tom Collins and Brandy Cooler.

34) Name the cocktail which is served in a conch shell.

Rum Sour.

35) Name the cocktail which is served in a copper mug.

Moscow Mule.

36) Name the cocktail with fried bacon as its garnish.

Mitch Morgan.

37) Name the cocktail which is served either in a pineapple shell or in a coconut shell.

Piña Colada.

38) Name the cocktail which means 'Strained Pineapple' in Spanish.

Piña Colada.

39) Name the cocktail which is named after a Scottish folk hero.

Rob Roy.

40) Name the cocktail named after two cartoon characters (served mainly during Christmas time).

Tom & Jerry.

41) What is the spirit used in Caipirinha cocktail?

Cachaça.

42) Which cocktail means Peasant's Drink?

Caipirinha.

43) What makes a Paloma cocktail?

Tequila and grapefruit soda.

44) The name of this cocktail comes from the Tahitian word for "good" or "excellence." Which cocktail are we talking about?

Mai-Tai.

45) Which famous Spanish cocktail means 'to bleed'?

Sangria.

46) Name the spirit used in Rob Roy cocktail.

Scotch whisky.

47) What is the garnish for Manhattan cocktail?

Maraschino cherry.

48) Name the cocktail which is named after Gerardo Machado, the Cuban President.

El Presidente.

49) Where was El Presidente cocktail born?

Havana, Cuba.

50) Which cocktail is named after a Hollywood bullfighter movie released in 1922?

Blood and Sand.

51) Name the most popular Drambuie based cocktail.

Rusty Nail.

52) This drink is the Puerto Rican version of Eggnog. Identify it.

Coquito.

53) Which liquor would you find in Zombie?

Rum.

54) Name the liquors used in a Long Island Iced Tea cocktail.

Gin, Vodka, Rum and Tequila.

55) What are the ingredients of Widow's Kiss cocktail?

Angostura bitter, Benedictine, Calvados and Yellow Chartreuse.

56) What is the name of the world's largest cocktail festival?

Tales of the cocktail held in New Orleans.

57) Name the cocktail served particularly to a group of people in a special ceramic bowl known as 'Volcanic Bowl.'

Flaming Volcano.

58) Which cocktail is named after the famous Scottish poet, Robert Burns?

Bobby Burns.

59) Which cocktail is named after an alleged World War II spy?

Brass Monkey.

60) Name two cocktails which were the favourites of Ernest Hemingway.

Daiquiri and Dry Martini.

61) Which cocktail is named after the writer, Ernest Hemingway?

Hemingway Daiquiri.

62) Name the cocktail created to mark the 80th birthday of Sir Winston Churchill.

Four Square.

63) Which cocktail is named after a cartoon character of Warner Bros.?

Bugs Bunny.

64) Name the cocktail created to mark the first moon landing of the mankind.

Moonwalk.

65) Which cocktail is believed to have been introduced by the East India Company (British) in India?

Gin & Tonic Cocktail (G&T).

66) Which cocktail was created by a Restaurant Manager to celebrate the grand opening of an Italian restaurant in Calgary, Canada?

Caesar Cocktail.

67) Name the cocktail which is traditionally served with a wooden muddler.

Dawa.

68) What is the meaning of 'Dawa'?

Swahili word 'Dawa' means something between a medicine and magic potion.

69) Name the cocktail which was first made in Harry's Bar at Venice and was named after Giovanni Bellini, a famous artist.

Bellini.

70) Which cocktail is made with Prosecco and peach purée?

Bellini.

71) Name the cocktail named after a Californian surfer who used to bang against the wall of the bar.

Harvey Wallbanger.

72) Who was the first to make 'Collins' cocktail?

John Collins.

73) Name the first cocktail to feature a sugar-crusted rim.

The Brandy Crusta.

74) What are the ingredients of Screw driver cocktail?

Vodka and orange juice.

75) Which cocktail's modification is Harvey Wallbanger?

Screwdriver cocktail.

76) Name the cocktail served in Singapore Airlines.

Singapore Sling.

77) Name the traditional spirit used in a Punch drink.

Rum.

78) Who is known as the 'Father of American Mixology'?

Jeremiah "Jerry" P.Thomas popularly known as Jerry Thomas.

79) Name six gin based cocktails.

Aviation, Dry Martini, Gimlet, Pink lady, Singapore Sling and White lady.

80) Name five vodka based cocktails.

Bloody Mary, Screw driver, Harvey Wallbanger, Salty Dog and Moscow mule.

81) Name four brandy based cocktails.

B&B, Between the Sheets, Brandy Alexander and Side car.

82) Name few whiskey based cocktails.

Manhattan, Godfather, Rusty Nail, Whisky Sour, Rob Roy, Sazerac etc.

83) Name six rum based cocktails.

Bacardi cocktail, Daiquiri, Mai Tai, Mojito, Piña colada and Planter's Punch.

84) Name few tequila based cocktails.

Tequila Sunrise, Margarita, Bull's Blood, Tequila Sunset, Brave Bull, Viva Villa etc.

85) Name four beer based cocktails.

Black Velvet, Depth Charge, Snake Bite and Shandy.

86) Name five wine based cocktails.

Bucks Fizz, Kir, Kir Royale, Sangria and Spritzer.

87) Give the names of four liqueur based cocktails.

Grasshopper, Godfather, Godmother and Widow's Kiss.

88) Name any two sake based cocktails.

Far Eastside and Saketini.

89) Mention any four baiju based cocktails.

Hong Kong Margarita.

90) Which drink was once known as 'Bucket of Blood'?

Bloody Mary.

91) What is Egg nog?

It's a traditional Christmas drink with rum or brandy along with milk.

92) Name the gin based cocktail which was once known as 'Pink Shimmy.'

Pink Lady.

93) Which cocktail was invented by Ernest Hemingway?

Death in the afternoon (Absinthe and Champagne).

94) Name the variant of Kir cocktail that substitutes white wine with Champagne.

Kir Royale (Champagne and Crème de cassis).

95) Name five champagne based cocktails.

Kir Royale, Bellini, French'75, Bucks Fizz and Champagne Cocktail.

96) Name three absinthe based cocktails.

Absinthe Frappé, Chrysanthemum and Death in the afternoon.

97) Which gin based cocktail is named after a Navy Surgeon?

Gimlet.

98) Which gin based cocktail is named after French 75mm field gun?

French 75.

99) Name the cocktail named after an aircraft and music band.

B 52.

100) Name the cocktail that features all three different styles of rum.

Zombie.

101) Name the cocktail which is also the name of a Rye whiskey brand in U.S.

Sazerac.

102) Which is the famous gin based cocktail named after the surgical grafting technique of monkey testicle tissue into humans?

The Monkey Gland.

103) Name one of the strongest cocktails in the world that hails from Alabama, named after a prostitute.

Aunt Roberta.

104) Name the cocktail that features maximum no. of liquors.

Long Island Iced Tea.

105) Which beer based cocktail was created to mourn the death of Prince Albert (1861)?

Black Velvet.

106) Name the cocktail that has pickled onion as its garnish.

Gibson.

107) Mention the names of three cocktails that have sweet vermouth as an ingredient

Manhattan, Rob Roy and Negroni.

108) What are the ingredients of Madras cocktail?

Absolut vodka, cranberry and orange juice.

109) Name the cocktail which is regarded as the first flaming cocktail of the world.

Blue Blazer.

110) Name the gin based cocktail named after a fictional character created by Scottish novelist J.M Barrie.

Peter Pan Cocktail. The cocktail features gin, orange juice, dry vermouth and bitters.

111) Name the cocktail created to mark the 90th birthday of Sir Winston Churchill.

The Blenheim.

112) Name few edible cocktail garnishes.

Maraschino cherry, Stuffed olive, Grapes, Slice of a pineapple without skin etc.

113) Name few non-edible cocktail garnishes.

Paper parasols, Straws, Cocktail sticks, Tooth picks, Swizzle sticks etc.

114) What are canned cocktails?

These are ready to drink cocktails available in cans.

115) Which Italian cocktail holds the title, 'King of Aperitvo cocktails'?

Negroni.

116) What is the cocktail version of iced tea?

Long Island Iced Tea.

117) Which rum based cocktail was born when the bartender decided to get rid of less popular local rum brands?

Hurricane.

118) Name the vodka based cocktail which is named after a peninsula located in United States, famous for cranberries.

Cape Codder.

119) What is the main difference between a Manhattan and Rob Roy cocktail?

Manhattan cocktail is made with rye whisky and Rob Roy is prepared with Scotch whisky.

120) What is the vodka version of gin based Martini?

Vodkatini.

121) Name the cocktail developed by the members of Royal Navy that features Plymouth gin and Angostura bitters.

Pink gin.

122) Which cocktail did James Bond invent through Ian Fleming?

Vesper.

123) Name the most famous Lillet cocktail.

Vesper.

124) What is Pimm's and after whom it is named?

Pimm's is a gin based collection of cocktails named after its creator James Pimm.

125) What is Pimm's no.1?

Pimm's no.1 is a gin based cocktail consisting of gin, herbs, spices and ginger ale.

126) What is the vegetarian substitute for egg white in cocktails?

Aquafaba/chickpea juice.

127) Who is regarded as the 'Godfather of bartending'?

Jerry Thomas.

128) What is Molecular mixology?

Molecular mixology is a concept evolved out of molecular gastronomy that involves creating cocktails with the help of science.

129) Name any three techniques that are involved in Molecular mixology.

Spherification, Emulsification and Suspension.

130) Which ingredient creates smoke in cocktails?

Liquid nitrogen and dry ice.

131) Is consuming liquid nitrogen fatal for humans?

Yes, it is fatal for humans as consuming low temperature liquid nitrogen can badly damage the tissues located in mouth and intestinal tract.

132) Name few ingredients applied in molecular mixology.

Gum acacia, soy lecithin, xantham gum, gelatin, agar-agar etc.

133) Name few chemicals used as part of molecular mixology.

Calcium chloride, calcium lactate, sodium alginate etc.

134) Give three examples for molecular mixology cocktails.

Mojito spheres, Molecular Mojito,

135) Why blow torches are used in mixology?

Blow torches are used in mixology to apply heat or fire on drinks.

5.3 Mocktails

1) What are Mocktails?

Mocktails are non-alcoholic beverages prepared by mixing different fruit juices, syrups and flavoured or plain aerated water.

2) Who was the first to use the word 'Mocktail'?

The word was first used by John Doxat in his book, 'The Complete Drinkers Companion' which was released by Grafton Books in the year 1985.

3) The term mocktail is a combination of two words. Which are those two words?

The words are 'mock' and 'cocktail.'

4) Which is the popular term used to denote 'virgin cocktails'?

Mocktails.

5) Who are the targeted customers for mocktails?

Children and teetotalers.

6) Which mocktail is believed to be the world's first mocktail?

Shirley Temple.

7) Give three examples for classic mocktails.

Shirley Temple, Roy Rogers and Cinderella.

8) Name the mocktail named after a child actress which features lemon-lime soda, ginger ale and grenadine syrup, garnished with maraschino cherry.

Shirley Temple mocktail.

9) Which famous mocktail is also referred as 'Virgin Sling'?

Shirley Temple mocktail.

10) Name the non-alcoholic version of the famous Bloody Mary cocktail.

Virgin Mary.

11) Which popular cocktail's mocktail version is Nojito/Virgin Mojito?

Mojito.

12) Which cola based mocktail is named after an American singer and actor?

Roy Rogers.

13) Name the mocktail which is known by the name 'Cherry Coke.'

Roy Rogers.

14) What are the ingredients of Fruit Punch mocktail?

Orange juice, pineapple juice, mango juice, grenadine syrup and ice cream.

15) Name a mocktail which is prepared in Punch bowl.

Fruit Punch mocktail.

16) What is the mocktail version of Piña colada called?

Coco colada/Virgin Piña colada.

17) Mention the juices used to prepare Cinderella mocktail.

Pineapple juice, orange juice and lemon juice.

18) Name the mocktail created by mixing lemonade and iced tea.

Arnold Palmer.

19) Name a mocktail prepared by the muddling process.

Nojito.

20) What are the ingredients of Virgin mudslide mocktail?

Cold coffee, chocolate syrup, hazelnut syrup, vanilla ice cream and cinnamon.

21) Which drink is named after the famous golfer?

Arnold Palmer.

22) Name the mocktail version of Tequila Sunrise cocktail.

Sweet Sunrise/Virgin Sunrise.

23) Which are the different methods followed to prepare mocktails?

They can be stirred, layered, build and shaken.

24) How mocktails are served?

Mocktails are served chilled in their appropriate glassware from the right hand side of the guest on top of a coaster. Straws are placed in a straw holder.

25) Name one mocktail which is served warm.

Virgin Hot Toddy.

5.4 Liqueurs

1) What are Liqueurs?

Liqueurs are spirits that are sweetened and flavoured with fruits, herbs, spices, flowers and nuts.

2) What is the difference between liquor and liqueur?

Liquors are distilled alcoholic beverages whereas liqueurs are sweetened and flavoured liquors.

3) From which word is liqueur derived?

The word liqueur comes from the Latin word 'lique-facre' which means 'to dissolve'.

4) How liqueurs are produced?

Liqueurs are produced by extracting the flavour from the base material through pressure/distillation/infusion or percolation.

5) Give few examples for liqueurs.

Amaretto, Chartreuse, Grand Marnier, Midori, Sheridan's etc.

6) How liqueurs are served?

Liqueurs are served neat, as frappe (over ice) and can be used as in ingredient in cocktails.

7) What is a liqueur trolley?

A trolley kept in restaurant with a wide display of liqueurs from around the world.

8) Classify liqueurs based on the category.

Generic liqueurs and Proprietary liqueurs.

9) What are Generic liqueurs?

Liqueurs that could be prepared by anyone using the available recipes are termed as Generic liqueurs.

10) What are Proprietary liqueurs?

Proprietary liqueurs refer to those liqueurs that have a secret recipe for its making and are patented products. The brand names of the liqueurs are registered and it forbids others to create a similar liqueur.

11) Give two examples for Generic liqueurs

Anisette and Crème de menthe.

12) Give two examples for Proprietary liqueurs.

Chartreuse (France) and Grand Marnier (France).

13) Classify liqueurs based on alcoholic strength and sugar content.

Classification	Alcoholic strength	Sugar content
Demi fine	40%	20 to 25% gms per litre
Fines	49%	40 to 45% gms per litre
Surfines	52%	45 to 50% gms per litre
Curad Sec	78%	45 to 50% gms per litre

14) Classify liqueurs based on the ingredients used for flavouring. Give examples.

Classification	Examples
Berry liqueurs	Chambord, Crème de cassis, Lakka and Sloe gin
Coffee liqueurs	Kahlua, Tia Maria, Café Rica and Kamora
Chocolate liqueurs	Crème de cacao and Sheridan's
Cream liqueurs	Bailey's Irish Cream (Ireland) and Feeney's Irish Cream (Ireland).
Crème liqueurs	Crème de cerise (cherry flavoured), Crème de framboise (raspberry flavoured), Crème de mûre (blackberry flavoured) and Crème de noyaux (almond flavoured)
Fruit liqueurs	Cointreau, Southern Comfort, Midori and Maraschino
Herbal liqueurs	Bénédictine, Drambuie, Gallliano and Unicum
Nut liqueurs	Amaretto, Crème de noyaux, Frangelico and Nocello

15) Who were the first to manufacture liqueurs commercially?

Monks and alchemists.

16) Name two liqueur recipes developed by monks.

Bénédictine and Chartreuse.

17) Which monk is said to have formulated the recipe of Bénédictine liqueur?

Don Bernardo Vincelli.

18) Name three famous citrus flavoured liqueurs.

Cointreau (France) and Curaçao (Caribbean islands of Curaçao) and Grand Marnier (France),

19) What is Cointreau?

Cointreau is a French brand of Triple Sec made from peel of bitter and sweet oranges.

20) What was the initial name of Cointreau?

Curaçao Blanco Triple Sec.

21) What is the colour of Cointreau?

Cointreau is colourless.

22) Name two versions of Cointreau.

Original and Blood Orange.

23) What is Curaçao?

Curaçao is a generic citrus liqueur made from drier peel of bitter oranges named Laraha seen in the Caribbean Island of Curaçao, Netherlands. Bols and De Kuyper are popular Curaçao brands.

24) What is the colour of Curaçao liqueur?

Curaçao liqueur comes in five colours-Blue, Orange, Red, Green and Transparent.

25) What is Triple Sec?

Triple Sec is a French orange flavoured liqueur similar to Curaçao.

26) Why Triple Sec is named so?

Triple Sec is termed so as it is distilled thrice. 'Sec' means dry.

27) What is Grand Marnier?

Grand Marnier is cognac based French liqueur that possesses the flavor of orange peel.

28) Which are the styles of Grand Marnier?

Grand Marnier Cordon Rouge and Grand Marnier Cordon Jaune.

29) Name few popular liqueur based cocktails

Black Russian, Harvey wallbanger, Margarita, B&B, Side car etc.

30) Name three generic liqueur brands.

Bols, De Kuyper and Luxardo.

31) When onwards liqueurs started to gain popularity?

In the beginning of 20th century.

32) Who were the first to preserve fruit in alcohol?

The Dutch.

33) When liqueurs could be served during a meal?

It could be served either as an aperitif or digestif.

34) Give few examples of liqueurs which could be served as aperitifs.

Cherry brandy, Cointreau and Crème de cassis.

35) Give few examples of liqueurs which could be served as digestifs.

Amarula, Galliano and Grand Marnier.

36) Give two examples for vegetable based liqueurs.

Cynar and Jägermeister.

37) Name the celery root based herbal liqueur from Chicago.

Apologue.

38) Give an example for ginger liqueur.

King's Ginger from Netherlands.

39) Name three coconut flavoured liqueurs.

Malibu (Barbados), Cocoribe (USA) and Tequipal Coconut liqueur (Mexico).

40) Name two cherry flavoured liqueurs.

Kirschwasser (Germany) and Maraschino (Italy).

41) Name two blueberry flavoured liqueurs.

Jerzynówka (Poland) and Minaki (Canada).

42) Name one black raspberry liqueur.

Chambord (France).

43) Name two passion fruit flavoured liqueurs.

Passoã (France) and Maracujá (Portugal).

44) Name two honey based liqueurs.

Krupnik (Poland) and Jack Daniel's (USA).

45) What is Van der hum?

A South African liqueur produced from the peel of naartjies fruit (tangerine flavour).

46) Name the banana liqueur manufactured by the famous Suntory distillery of Japan.

Lena.

47) Which liqueur is considered as the Irish equivalent of Glen Mist?

Irish Mist.

48) Which chocolate liqueur is named after the famous Lady Godiva of England?

Godiva (Belgium).

49) Name one herbal liqueur from Mexico.

Damiana.

50) Which is the Damiana flower infused tequila liqueur?

Agavero.

51) Name a cactus liqueur.

Agavero.

52) Name the first liqueur manufactured in Ireland.

Irish Mist.

53) Name the most famous coconut flavoured liqueur in the world.

Malibu.

54) Name the green tea liqueur produced by Suntory, Japan.

Zen.

55) Name the French citrus liqueur which literally means 'Perfect Love'

Parfait Amour/Parfait d'Amour.

56) Which liqueur means 'the drink that satisfies'?

Drambuie.

57) Name the Canadian cherry liqueur which literally means 'Caged Love.'

Amour en Cage.

58) What is the relevance of the term 'D.O.M' which appears on the label of Bénédictine bottle?

'D.O.M' stands for 'Deo Optimo Maximo' which means 'To God, Most Good, Most Great'.

59) Name the Italian liqueur manufactured in Venice and is popularly known as 'the greatest cherry liqueur of all times.'

Maraschino.

60) Name the liqueur which is said to be the favourite liqueur of Louis XIV.

Chambord (France).

61) Name the liqueur bottle designed like a 'friar' with a white chord around its waist.

Frangelico (Italy).

62) Name the liqueur which is sold in Mexican pyramid shaped bottle.

Xanath.

63) Name the liqueur named after 'Brother Angelico.'

Frangelico (Italy).

64) Name the liqueur brand that features a sunset behind two palm trees on its white bottle.

Malibu.

65) Name the most famous coconut liqueur brand in the world.

Malibu.

66) What is Chartreuse?

An ancient liqueur from France made by Carthusian monks by combining liquor and 130 herbal extracts is Chartreuse.

67) How many types of Chartreuse exist?

Two types-Green and Yellow, Green having more alcoholic content, drier than the latter.

68) Name two anise based liqueurs.

Anisette and Unicum

69) What is Anisette?

Anisette is anise/sweet cumin based liqueur.

70) Which is the most popular way of consuming Anisette?

By adding water to it.

71) Name the popular Italian Anisette.

Sambuca.

72) Which is the aniseed liqueur made from the sap of mastic tree?

Mastika/Mastiha from Greece.

73) What is Cherry Heering?

Cherry Heering is a brand of cherry liqueur currently owned by De Kuyper. The recipe of the liqueur dates back to 1818.

74) Name the mint used traditionally to flavour Crème de menthe.

Corsican mint.

75) Which liqueur is traditionally associated with Crêpes Suzette?

Grand Marnier.

76) What are the different flavours launched by Malibu brand other than coconut?

Banana, Lime, Mango, Passion fruit, Pineapple and Strawberry.

77) Name the Italian liqueur which means '100 herbs'

Centerbe, a herbal liqueur.

78) Which liqueur features thin flakes of 23 carat gold leaves in it?

Danziger Goldwasser from Germany

79) What is the meaning of Goldwasser?

It means 'gold water.'

80) Name the best selling Lychee fruit liqueur in the world.

Soho (France).

81) Which is the popular Hungarian herbal liqueur made by the beverage company Zwack?

Unicum.

82) What was 'Southern Comfort' liqueur originally known as?

Cuffs and Buttons.

83) Name the toffee flavoured liqueur from Germany.

Dooleys.

84) Which Italian herbal liqueur means 'gold' in Latin?

Aurum.

85) Name the sweet, pale gold coloured, orange flavoured liqueur from Italy.

Aurum.

86) Which liqueur brand bottle is shaped after a wine flask excavated at Pompei, Italy?

Aurum.

87) Name the popular coffee flavoured liqueur from Costa-Rica.

Café Rica.

88) What is Salmiakki Koskenkorva?

A pre-mixed Finnish liqueur made from vodka and liquorice flavoured with salt.

89) Name the South African liqueur made from marula fruit.

Amarula.

90) What is Get 27?

A generic brand of crème de menthe.

91) Name the Italian equivalent of Grand Marnier.

Gran Gala.

92) Which Japanese liqueur is made from 'ume' fruit?

Umeshu or The Choya.

93) Name the Austrian chocolate liqueur named after Salzburg's most famous son.

Mozart.

94) Name the famous Belgium chocolate liqueur named after a naked lady.

Godiva.

95) Name the sweet rum based liqueur from Jamaica produced by Wray and Nephew.

Rumona.

96) Which liqueur from Jamaica is named after 'Aunt Maria'?

Tia Maria.

97) Which coffee liqueur brand is known as 'The Champagne of Maine'?

Allen's Coffee Brandy.

98) What is Becherovka?

Becherovka from Czech Republic is a bitter liqueur made from 32 herbs.

99) What is the base of Patrón XO Café liqueur?

The base is Patrón Silver tequila.

100) Name one date liqueur from Israel.

Tamara.

101) Which is the world's best selling liqueur (as of 2020)?

Baileys.

102) Which liqueur brand has launched its red-velvet flavour?

Baileys.

103) Name the world's best selling coffee liqueur.

Kahlúa.

104) What is Kahlúa?

Kahlúa is coffee flavoured rum from Mexico.

105) Which coffee beans are used in Kahlúa?

Coffee Arabica.

106) What is the meaning of the word Kahlúa?

It means "Heart of the Veracruz people."

107) Name two cocktails made with Kahlúa.

Black Russian and Espresso Martini.

108) Name the first cocktail to use Kahlúa as an ingredient.

Black Russian.

109) Where is Jägermeister liqueur produced?

Germany.

110) What is the meaning of the word, 'Jägermeister'?

Master Hunter.

111) How many botanicals are used in the making of Jägermeister?

56.

112) Name few ingredients used in Jägermeister.

Licorice, saffron, citrus peel, poppy seeds etc.

113) Which Saint's story is said to have inspired the famous Jägermeister trademark?

The story of Saint Hubertus.

114) Name two saints of hunters who are associated with Jägermeister.

Saint Hubertus and Saint Eustace.

115) Which is the only one flavor of Jägermeister available other than its original?

Ginger lime.

116) Name the poet whose poetic verses are featured on the back label of Jägermeister bottle.

Oskar von Riesenthal

117) Name the Japanese liqueur brand that comes in a glowing green bottle.

Ty Ku citrus liqueur.

118) Name one example for sake and soju based liqueur.

Sake based – Gekkeikan Kirei Momoshu (Japan).

Soju based – Ty Ku (Japan).

119) Mention six liqueurs with its name, country of origin, base spirit, flavouring and colour.

Name of the liqueur	Country	Base spirit	Flavouring	Colour
Amarula	South Africa	Fruit spirit base	Creamy caramel, spices	Peach
Bailey's Irish Cream	Ireland	Irish whiskey	Honey, Chocolate	Golden yellow

Continued…

Cointreau	France	Neutral spirit	Orange	Clear
Kahlúa	Mexico	Neutral spirit	Coffee	Brown
Sambuca	Italy	Neutral spirit	Licorice	Clear
Sheridan's	Ireland	Irish whiskey	White chocolate and coffee	White & Brown

120) Which liqueur is often referred to as 'Mother/Queen of all liqueurs'?

Chartreuse.

121) Name the different process involved in liqueur making.

Distillation, percolation, infusion and maceration.

122) Which yellow coloured sweet, herbal liqueur is named after an Italian hero, Giuseppe Galliano?

Galliano.

123) Name the rum based liqueur that means 'delicious' in Spanish and inspired by Horchata.

Ricura.

124) Which liqueur was once marketed as a liqueur for genteel ladies?

Southern Comfort.

125) This liqueur is said to have been first made by witches disguised as maidens. Identify this Italian liqueur.

Strega.

126) Name the diet friendly version of Baileys Original Irish Cream.

Baileys Deliciously Light.

127) Which two liqueur bottles are designed after globus cruciger?

Chambord and Forbidden fruit.

128) Which liqueur was created for Napoleon Bonaparte?

Mandarine Napoléon (orange flavoured liqueur from Belgium).

129) What is the shelf life of fruit liqueurs once the bottle is opened?

It should be consumed within 6 months.

130) What is the shelf life of egg and cream based liqueurs once the bottle is opened?

It should be refrigerated and consumed within 8 weeks.

5.5 Liquors

1) What is Liquor?

The word liquor refers to all types of alcoholic beverages that undergo distillation process.

2) From which word did the word 'whisky' originate?

The word 'whisky' originated from the Gaelic expression, 'uisge beatha' or 'usquebaugh' which means 'water of life'.

3) What is the base of whisky?

Grains such as barley, rye, corn, maize, wheat etc.

4) What are the different types of whisky?

Scotch, Bourbon, Tennessee, Irish, Canadian, Rye, Japanese, Indian etc.

5) What is the difference between 'whisky' and 'whiskey'?

The word 'whisky' is seen on the labels of whisky bottles produced in Scotland and other countries whereas Americans and Irish people use the term 'whiskey.'

6) Why there exists difference in spellings of whisky?

It's mainly because of the Scottish and Irish Gaelic translations.

7) Name different types of whisky based on its country of origin and give four brand names for each.

Name	Country of origin	Brand names
Scotch whisky	Scotland	Glenfiddich, Glenlivet, Glenmorangie and Dewar's.
Irish whiskey	Ireland	Bushmills, Jameson, Powers and Tullamore Dew.
Bourbon whiskey	America	Jim Beam, Maker's Mark, Four Roses and Knob Creek.
Tennessee whiskey	America	Jack Daniel's, George Dickel and Benjamin Prichard's.
American Rye whiskey	America	Elijah Craig, Rossville Union, Old Overholt and New Riff.

Canadian whisky	Canada	Crown Royal, Canadian Club, Black Velvet and Pendelton.
Japanese whisky	Japan	The Yamazaki, Hibiki, The Chita and Toki.
Indian whisky	India	Amrut Fusion, Paul John, Rampur and McDowell's No.1.

8) What is the plural for whisky and whiskey?

Singular	*Plural*
Whisky	Whiskies
Whiskey	Whiskeys

9) Can Bourbon whiskey be made anywhere in America?

Yes.

10) Where are majority of Bourbon whiskeys made in America?

In the State of Kentucky.

11) Which spirit is referred to as America's native spirit?

Bourbon whiskey.

12) What gives Bourbon whiskey its sweet flavor?

Corn.

13) Name two types of barrels used for aging whisky/whiskey.

Charred oak and used sherry casks.

14) What are the stipulations laid by American Bourbon Association for a whiskey to be called 'bourbon'?

- ➤ The mash, which is a mix of grains, should contain at least 51% of corn.

- ➤ Whiskey should be aged in new charred oak barrels without the addition of any additives or colourings.

- ➤ While bottling, bourbon should have a minimum of 40% ABV.

15) What is a Straight Bourbon whiskey?

Bourbon whiskey which is aged in the new oak barrels for at least two years is referred to as Straight Bourbon whiskey.

16) What is the significance of the term 'Kentucky Bourbon' on a whiskey label?

It means that the particular Bourbon whiskey has been distilled and aged in Kentucky State of America.

17) Who is regarded as the 'Father of Bourbon' whiskey?

Elijah Craig.

18) Who was the first to age Bourbon whiskey in newly charred oak barrels?

Rev.Elijah Craig, a Baptist preacher.

19) What does the term 'white whiskey' (white dog) refer to?

Unaged whiskey.

20) What is American Rye whiskey?

Rye whiskey produced in America from a mash of 51% rye is termed as American Rye whiskey.

21) What is 'sour mash'?

A fermented mash of previous fermentation.

22) Who was the first to try out the 'sour mash' process?

James C.Jim Crow

23) What does the term 'Bottled in Bond' mean?

It means that the distilled product should be stored in federal warehouses for a period of four years under strict supervision by the government officials.

24) How bourbon whiskey gets its colour?

It gains colour from the barrels in which it is stored.

25) From where does the word 'bourbon' come from?

It comes from the French royalty, the House of Bourbon.

26) What are the differences between 'charring' and 'toasting' the oak barrels?

Criteria of differentiation	Charring	Toasting
Process	Faster	Slower
Level of penetration	Heat doesn't enter the wood	Heat gets deep into the wood

Continued…

Colour	Dark	Light
Flavour	Sweet, more vanilla and tannin	Spicy, vanilla flavour

27) Name the process by which the interior wood of cask gets converted into caramelised sugars.

Charring.

28) What is Tennessee whiskey?

Tennessee whiskey is a light brown coloured American whiskey that comes from the Tennessee region.

29) Which is the world's no.1 selling American whiskey brand?

Jack Daniel's.

30) Name the world's best selling whiskey brand (as per June 2020).

Jack Daniel's.

31) Which step differentiates Tennessee whiskey from Bourbon whiskey?

Lincoln County Process.

32) What is Lincoln County Process?

The whiskies are filtered through a thick layer of charcoal (made from the wood of the sugar maple tree) before being put into cask. This step is known as Charcoal mellowing and is carried out for around 7 to 10 days.

33) In which part of Tennessee is Jack Daniel's distillery located at?

Lynchburg.

34) What are the ingredients of Jack Daniel's whiskey?

Corn, rye, malted barley, water and yeast.

35) How does Jack Daniel's whiskey get its colour and flavour?

From the barrel.

36) Name the oldest registered distillery in America.

Jack Daniel's.

37) How much percentage of corn is present in George Dickel Tennessee whiskey?

84% Corn.

38) Which company owns George Dickel Tennessee whiskey?

Diageo.

39) Name the only whiskey brand which does not follow Lincoln County Process but still called as Tennessee whiskey.

Prichard's Tennessee whiskey.

40) What was the real name of Jack Daniel?

Jack's real name was Jasper Newton Daniel.

41) Name the first country to legislate an age requirement for whisky.

Canadian whisky.

42) Which Bourbon whiskey brand is sold in square bottles that are sealed with red wax?

Maker's Mark.

43) What is Canadian whisky?

Canadian whisky is a type of whisky produced in Canada and is made from cereal grains. It is mostly blended.

44) Name the grains used to make Canadian whisky.

Corn, malted barley, rye and wheat.

45) What is the minimum ageing period for a Canadian whisky?

Three years.

46) Name three brands of South African whisky.

Three Ships, Copper Republic and Bain's Cape Mountain.

47) Name South Africa's first grain whisky.

Bain's Cape Mountain.

48) What is Irish whiskey?

Irish whiskey is whiskey produced and matured in Ireland, made from malted and unmalted barley along with very small quantities of other grains (maize, rye, millet etc.).

49) What are some of the main differences between Irish whiskey and Scotch whisky?

Criteria of differentiation	Irish whiskey	Scotch whisky
Country of origin	Ireland	Scotland
Base	Malted and unmalted barley with very small quantities of other grains.	Malted barley
Still used	Pot still and Patent still	Pot still
No. of distillations	Thrice	Twice
Period for maturation	Five years in casks	Three years in casks
Peat and Charcoal	No	Yes. Gives smoky flavour.
Spelling	Whiskey	Whisky

50) What is Poteen?

A term used to denote illicitly made whiskey in Ireland.

51) Name the biggest producer of whisky in the world.

Scotland.

52) Name the association that promotes, protects and represents the interests of the whisky industry in Scotland and around the world.

SWA (Scotch Whisky Association).

53) What is Scotch whisky?

Scotch whisky is the short form for Scottish whisky and is a quality whisky produced in Scotland by the Scots.

54) What makes Scotch whisky superior to other whiskeys/whiskies?

The final flavor and quality of the Scotch whisky is unmatchable and it largely relies on the type of cereal used, the malting process, the peat used, the water used, the skills of the distiller and the blender.

55) Name three ingredients need to produce Scotch?

Grains, water and yeast.

56) Which are the main two types of Scotch whisky?

Malt whisky and Grain whisky.

57) What is malt whisky?

Scotch malt whisky is a kind of whisky made entirely from malted barley.

58) What is grain whisky?

Grain whisky is made from a mixed of cereals (maize, wheat, millet) and malted barley.

59) Which are the five whisky producing regions of Scotland?

Campbeltown, Highlands, Islay, Lowlands and Speyside.

60) Give the character and whisky brands produced in different Scotch whisky regions.

Name of the region	Character	Brands
Campbeltown	Heavy and smoky flavoured	Glen Scotia, Gglengyle and Springbank
Highlands	Light and refined, slightly smoky and full flavoured	Dalmore, Glenmorangie and Oban
Islay	Strong peaty flavour	Ardbeg, Bowmore and Lagavulin
Lowlands	Light and less smoky character	Auchentoshan, Daftmill and Girvan
Speyside	Sweet and fruity character	Glenfarclas, Glenfiddich and The Macallan

61) Which Scottish whisky region was once known as the 'Victorian Whisky Capital of the world'?

Campbeltown.

62) Name the whisky region that produces whiskies with floral characteristics known as 'Lowland ladies.'

Lowlands.

63) Which is the largest Scotch whisky producing region?

Highlands.

64) Name the 'Malt Whisky Capital of the World.'

Dufftown.

65) What is Single malt whisky?

Single malt whisky is the product of a single distillery and is entirely made from malted barley. It is also known as Straight malt whisky.

66) What is Straight grain whisky?

A whisky made from either from a grain or a mix of grains but without malted barley is termed as Straight grain whisky. It's a product of a single distillery.

67) What is Blended whisky?

Blended whisky is a whisky produced by mixing malt and grain whiskies together. The role of blend master is crucial in deciding the ratio.

68) What is Vatted malt whisky?

This whisky is a blend of single malt whiskies from different distilleries.

69) What is Deluxe blend scotch whisky?

This kind of whisky is also blended but with higher proportion of malt whiskies than grain whiskies.

70) When is World Whisky Day observed?

It's observed on the Third Saturday of May every year.

71) What is Dram?

A single serve of whisky is Dram. It's mostly 45 ml.

72) This triangular shaped Scotch whisky bottle represents the three pillars of whisky making namely air, water and barley. Identify the brand.

Glenfiddich.

73) As per the law, for how long Scotch whisky must be aged in oak barrels?

For a minimum of three years.

74) Which style of Johnnie Walker is said to be Sir Winston Churchill's favourite of all?

Johnnie Walker Red Label.

75) Name the drink created by the Johnnie Walker team to honour 'Winston Churchill Day' on 9th of April 2014.

'Winston Walker' comprising of Johnnie Walker whisky, water and cinnamon sticks.

76) Which was the female version of Johnnie Walker launched on account of International Women's Day 2018?

Jane Walker.

77) Differentiate malt whisky from grain whisky.

Criteria of differentiation	Malt whisky	Grain whisky
Base	Malted barley	Grains
Still used	Pot still	Patent still

78) Name the Scotch whisky brand that has its label pasted at an angle of 24°.

Johnnie Walker.

79) Which famous Scotch whisky brand has the logo of the 'striding man'?

Johnnie Walker.

80) Why there is different colour codes for Johnnie Walker blended scotch whiskies?

The different colour code indicates different flavours of the whisky.

81) What was Johnnie Walker whisky originally known as?

Walker's Kilmarnock whisky.

82) Which is the most expensive Johnnie Walker label?

Johnnie Walker Blue Label.

83) Expand J&B in J&B Scotch whisky.

Justerini & Brooks.

84) Which Scotch whisky brand is the favourite of Captain Haddock and Snowy, two characters that appear in Hergé's comic named Tintin?

Loch Lomond.

85) Name the dogs featured in the label of Black & White blended Scotch whisky.

A black Scottish terrier and a West Highland white terrier.

86) Why many Single Malt Scotch whiskies start their names with 'glen'?

The meaning of the word 'glen' is valley. Many of the Scottish distilleries are named based on its location.

87) Give the names of few Single malt Scotch whisky brands and its meanings.

Brand name	Meaning
Glenfarclas	Valley of the green grass
Glenfiddich	Valley of the deer
Glenlivet	Valley through which river Livet flows
Glenmorangie	Valley of calm
Glen Scotia	Valley of Scots

88) Which blended Scotch whisky brand feature a tea clipper ship on its label?

Cutty Sark.

89) Name two casks used to age Scotch whisky.

Fresh or reused sherry oak casks and bourbon oak casks.

90) Which company is the world's largest Scotch whisky producer?

Diageo.

91) Name the Scotch whisky brand which will be launching its whisky in paper bottles in 2021.

Johnnie Walker.

92) Name the Scotch whisky brand that features Scotland's national game bird on its label.

Scotland's national game bird is the red grouse and the brand is The Famous Grouse.

93) Which is the strongest single malt whisky in the world?

Bruichladdich X4 Quadrupled whisky (92% ABV) from Islay, Scotland.

94) Identify the Scotch whisky brand which is referred to as "the King's own whisky."

Royal Brackla.

95) Which Scottish distillery did a study on the effects of gravity on whisky maturation by sending its whisky into outer space?

Ardbeg distillery.

96) Name the first ever Scotch distillery to be granted a Royal Warrant by King William IV?

Royal Brackla.

97) Which Islay distillery received a Royal Warrant from Prince Charles in 1994?

Laphroaig distillery.

98) How Vat 69 got its name?

The blend from Vat no.69 was once selected by the whisky experts and hence the name.

99) Which is world's first AI whisky?

Mackmyra whisky, a Swedish whisky brand.

100) Name few single malt Indian whiskies.

Amrut, Rampur and Paul John.

101) Which is India's first single malt whisky?

Amrut.

102) Which Indian single malt whisky secured no.3 position in Jim Murray's Whisky Bible of 2010?

Amrut Fusion.

103) Name the Indian single malt whisky that secured third position in Jim Murray's Whisky Bible of 2021.

John Paul Mithuna.

104) Which is the world's largest selling single pot still Irish whiskey?

Redbreast.

105) Name the first whisky brand in the world to be made from Hopi blue corn.

Balcones Baby Blue Corn Whisky, US.

106) Which popular show in HBO is the inspiration behind White Walker of Johnnie Walker?

Game of Thrones.

107) How whisky is served?

Whisky is at its best when served neat, but personal preferences dictates whether it is served on the rocks, with ice water, mineral water or with mixers such as lemonade and tonic water.

108) What is IMFL?

IMFL stands for Indian Made Foreign Liquor. The term refers to all the hard liquors such as vodka, gin, rum, whisky, brandy etc. produced in India.

109) Which is the most popular IMFL in India?

Whisky.

110) Give three brand names for Indian whiskies.

Officer's Choice, McDowell's No.1 and Royal Stag.

111) What is 'Eau-de-vie'?

'Eau-de-vie' is a general term used to denote brandy made from different fruits other than grapes.

112) Who were the first to make 'Eau-de-vie'?

Monks.

113) What is the meaning of the French expression, 'Eau-de-vie'?

'Eau-de-vie' means 'Water of Life.'

114) Name three countries where 'Eau-de-vie' is produced

France, Canada and United States.

115) Name few fruits used to make 'Eau-de-vie.'

Apple, Black currant, Cherry, Plum, Raspberry, Strawberry etc.

116) Give examples for 'Eau-de-vie.'

Calvados (Apple brandy), Fraise (Strawberry brandy), Framboise (Raspberry brandy), Kirschwasser/Kirsch (Cherry Brandy), Poire Williams (Pear brandy), Prunelle (Sloe Plum/Black thorn), Mirabelle (Yellow Plum brandy), Slivovitz (Black Plum brandy) etc.

117) Is 'Eau-de-vie' aged?

No, 'Eau-de-vie' is generally not aged though few exceptions are there.

118) When 'Eau-de-vie' could be served during a meal?

Since 'Eau-de-vie' is an excellent digestif, it's ideal to serve it during the end of a meal.

119) Name the pear variety used in the making of Poire 'eau de vie.'

Bartlett pear.

120) Which is the famous 'eau-de-vie' made from Dalmatian marasca cherries?

Maraschino.

121) Name the Hungarian 'eau-de-vie' made from apricots.

Barack pálinka.

122) What is Williamine?

Williamine is a famous brand of Poire brandy.

123) Give the names of two producers of 'Eau-de-vie.'

G.E Massenez from France and Clear Creek from United States.

124) What is Brandy?

Brandy is distilled alcoholic beverage made from fermented grape juice.

125) Which distilled alcoholic beverage is termed as 'Delightful soul of wine'?

Brandy.

126) From which word did brandy derive?

The term brandy is derived from the Dutch word 'brandewijn' which means 'burnt wine.'

127) Name the first country to produce brandy.

France.

128) Classify brandy.

Fruit brandy, grape brandy and pomace brandy.

129) What is Fruit brandy (Eau-de-vie)?

Brandy made from fermenting fruit other than grapes. Apples, plums, peaches, cherries, raspberries, blackberries, and apricots are the most commonly used fruits. Examples are Calvados, Kirsch, Poire Williams etc.

130) What is Grape brandy?

Brandy distilled from fermented grape juice or crushed but not pressed grape pulp and skin. This spirit is aged in wooden casks and the famous examples include Cognac and Armagnac.

131) What is Pomace brandy?

Brandy made from the pressed grape pulp, skins, and stems that remain after the grapes are crushed and pressed to extract most of the juice for wine. Examples are Italian Grappa and French Marc.

132) What is Cognac?

Cognac is the most famous brandy in the world that comes from the Cognac region of France.

133) 'All Cognacs are brandies but all brandies aren't Cognacs.' Explain the statement.

It states that only the brandy which is produced in the Cognac region of France could be called as Cognac.

134) How many grapes are legally permitted to be used in the making of Cognac? Name them.

Eight. Ugni Blanc, Folle Blanche, Colombard, Belzac Blanc, Blanc Ramé, Bouilleaux, Chalosse and Jurançon.

135) Name the three popular grape varieties used in the making of Cognac.

Ugni Blanc, Folle Blanche and Colombard.

136) What is wrong with the white wine used to distill Cognac?

The white wine obtained is not regarded as a good table wine as it is low in alcohol and high in acidity. But it produces Cognac of excellent quality.

137) Give the exact location of Cognac production.

It is made in the north of Bordeaux in the departments of Charente and the Charente Maritime in south-west France.

138) How many crus or designated areas are there for Cognac production? Name them.

Seven crus. Grande Champagne, Petite Champagne, Borderies, Fins Bois, Bons Bois, Bois Ordinaires and Bois Commune.

139) What is the type of soil seen in Cognac district?

Chalk.

140) What is Alambic Charentaise?

The copper pot still used for Cognac production.

141) What is brouillis (boiling up)?

The first distillate with an alcoholic content of 30%.

142) What is bonne chauffe (good heat)?

The second distillate with an alcohol content of up to 72%.

143) Name the casks used for ageing Cognac.

Limousine oak casks and Troncais oak casks.

144) What happens to Cognac during its period of ageing?

The colourless Cognac acquires colour (pale brown to dark brown), gains tannin and flavour.

145) What is Angel's Share/Part des anges?

While ageing, the porous wood allows a little oxidation and 2-3% of alcohol is lost through evaporation per year. This is known as Angel's Share/Part des anges and enables the Cognac to develop its character.

146) Name the microscopic fungus seen over Cognac during the Angel's Share process.

Torula compniacensis.

147) What are the different terms used on a Cognac label?

Terms	Explanation
Three star (***) /VS (Very Special) Cognac	The youngest cognac in the blend must be aged for at least two years in the barrel.
VSOP (Very Superior Old Pale)/ Vieux/Rare/Reserve/Royal	The youngest cognac in the blend must be aged for at least four years in the barrel.
X.O. (Extra Old), V.O (Very Old), Napoléon, Très Vieille Réserve, Héritage, Excellence, Suprême	The youngest cognac in the blend must be aged for at least six years in the barrel.
Hors d'âge (Beyond Age), Extra, Ancestral, Impérial ou Gol	The youngest cognac in the blend must be aged for at least ten years in the barrel.

148) What is Grande Fine Champagne Cognac?

This is a cognac made exclusively from grapes grown in the Grande Champagne zone in France.

149) What is Fine Champagne Cognac?

This is made from grapes grown in the Grande Champagne and Petite Champagne zones. The Cognac will contain at least 50% of the grapes from Grande Champagne zone.

150) Who is Maître de chai?

Maître de chai is a French term for master taster who is responsible for creating a unique Cognac blend.

151) What is Paradis?

It's a special cellar room where the aged cognacs are stored.

152) Name two glasses used to serve Cognac.

Brandy snifter and Wobble glass.

153) Give two mixers for Cognac.

Water and soda.

154) Mention six brand names of Cognac.

Remy Martin, Martell, Hennessy, Courvoisier, Camus and Bisquit.

155) Name the only brandy which is distilled twice in a pot still.

Cognac.

156) On an average, how many wine bottles are needed to produce one bottle of Cognac?

Ten.

157) What is Armagnac?

Armagnac is the world's oldest brandy that comes from the Armagnac region, Gascony of Southern France.

158) Name the distinctive flat bottles in which Armagnac is traditionally sold.

Basquaise.

159) During a meal, when can we serve Armagnac?

Traditionally, Armagnac is served at the end of a meal and is regarded as a digestif.

160) Name the distinctive patent still used in the production of Armagnac.

Alembic armagnaçaise.

161) How many grapes are legally permitted to be used in Armagnac production?

Ten.

162) Which are the main four grape varieties used in Armagnac production?

Folle Blanche, Ugni Blanc, Colombard and Bacco 22A.

163) Name the black oak cask used to age Armagnac.

Monlezun oak casks.

164) Mention five brand names of Armagnac.

Darroze, Gelos, Sempe, Janneau and Delord.

165) Differentiate Cognac from Armagnac.

Criteria of differentiation	Cognac	Armagnac
Region	Cognac	Armagnac
Type of still used	Pot still	Patent still
No. of distillation	Twice	Once
Cask used	Limousin or Troncais casks	Monlezun black oak casks
Price	Costlier than Armagnac	Cheaper than Cognac

166) What is Calvados?

Calvados is apple brandy made from fermented apple juice or obtained from a combination of apple and pear. Calvados can be served as an apéritif, blended in drinks, consumed between meals, as a digestif or with coffee. It is mainly produced in Normandy region of France.

167) Give five examples for fruit brandies with its flavour and country of origin.

Fruit brandy	Flavour	Country of origin
Abricotine	Apricot	Switzerland
Framboise	Raspberry	France
Poire Williams	Pear	France
Quetsch	Quetsch plums	France
Slivovitz	Plums	Yugoslavia

168) What is Pomace brandy?

Pomace brandy is a distilled alcoholic beverage made from the left overs of wine making. It contains the skins, pulp, seeds and stems of the fruit which is later fermented and distilled.

169) Give pomace brandy from different countries.

Name of the brandy	Country
Marc	France
Grappa	Italy
Orujo	Spain
Chacha	Georgia
Tsipouro	Greece

170) What is Pisco?

Pisco is a grape brandy that comes from Chile and Peru.

171) What is the precursor of Gin?

Genever.

172) What is Genever?

Genever (Dutch Gin) is a kind of liquor that hails from Holland and is basically made from 'moutwijn' or 'malt wine' (a mixture of malted barley, wheat, corn and rye).It possesses the characteristics of malt whisky and is a full-bodied white spirit. The alcohol content of Genever varies from 35%-38% ABV.

173) Which country's national liquor is Genever?

Genever is the national liquor of two countries, namely Belgium and Netherlands.

174) Which are the two styles of Genever?

Old and Young.

175) Differentiate Old Genever from Young Genever

Old Genever is generally aged in wooden barrels and has high malt content. It has a minimum of 15% malt wine and is crafted according to the 16th century distilling practices.

Young Genever is a much lighter version of Old Genever and is crafted according to the 19th century distilling practices. It could have a maximum of 15% malt wine and hence low malt content.

176) What is Grain Genever/Graanjenever?

Grain Genever is a term used to denote Genever which is distilled from 100% grain.

177) Give five well known brands of Genever.

Bokma, Bols, Diep 9, Old Duff and Olifant.

178) How Genever is served in bars?

Genever is served neat in tulip glasses either chilled or in room temperature. Few prefer to have it with bitters.

179) How Genever was marketed traditionally?

It used to be sold in handcrafted clay jugs.

180) What is Gin?

Gin is a distilled alcoholic beverage flavoured with botanicals.

181) What is the base of gin?

Grains such as wheat, barley and rye.

182) Name the base of modern gins.

Potato, grape

183) Name the primary flavouring agent used in Gin.

The primary flavouring agent used in Gin is Juniper berry. It imparts piney, spicy and citrus flavor to gin.

184) What is Juniper berry?

Juniper berry is a blue-green berry of the juniper plant mainly grown in Northern Italy, Croatia and United States.

185) What are Botanicals?

Botanical is a term used to denote roots, bark, branches, stem, leaves, fruits etc. of a plant.

186) Give few examples for botanicals used in making gin

Juniper berries, coriander seeds, caraway seeds, lemon peel, angelica root, star anise etc.

187) Which is the 'Birthplace of Gin'?

It's widely believed that Holland is the birthplace of gin.

188) Who is regarded as the 'Father of Gin'?

Many consider Franciscus de la Boe (Dr. Sylvius) as the 'Father of Gin'.

189) Give few nicknames of Gin

'Dutch Courage', 'Mother's Ruin' and 'Hollands'.

190) What are the different kinds of Gin available in the market?

London Dry, Plymouth, Old Tom, Dutch and New Western.

191) Which is the most famous style of gin?

London Dry.

192) What is London dry gin?

London dry gin is a style of gin which could be made anywhere in the world. It's a quality process designation that determines the final flavor of gin.

193) What is Plymouth gin?

Plymouth Gin is one type of gin which is produced only in the town of Plymouth, England. It is much drier and has earthy flavor than London Dry gin.

194) Name the English gin that had enjoyed the status of Geographical Indication once.

Plymouth Gin.

195) Where is Plymouth Gin distillery located?

It is located in the town of Plymouth, England.

196) What was Plymouth Gin distillery previously known as?

It was known as Black Friars Distillery.

197) What is the name of the ship that is seen in the label of a Plymouth Gin bottle?

Mayflower.

198) What is 'Navy Strength' Plymouth Gin?

It refers to Plymouth Gin that possesses an alcoholic strength of 57% ABV. (as per the alcoholic strength demanded by the British Royal Navy).

199) Name the oldest English distillery still in operation in its original location

Plymouth Gin distillery.

200) What is Old Tom Gin?

A style of gin sweeter than London dry gin.

201) What is New Western Gin?

Modern gins produced in U.S and other countries that emphasize less on juniper flavor.

202) What is Sloe Gin?

A gin based red coloured liqueur made using sloe berries (fruit of black thorn bush).

203) What is the normal colour of gin?

Colourless/Transparent.

204) What is Colour changing gin?

A blue coloured gin that changes its colour when an ingredient (lemonade or tonic water) is added to it.

205) Name the first hemp craft gin of India

Gin Gin (Goa).

206) Which Indian gin is blue in colour?

Clearly Good gin from Goa (colour from butterfly pea flower).

207) Which gin brand's bottle comes with the picture of tough Yeomen warders who guard the Tower of London?

Beefeater.

208) Name the gin which is sold in apothecary-style bottles.

Hendrick's.

209) Which gin bottle is designed after the shape of a cocktail shaker?

Tanqueray.

210) What is the significance of no. '24' in Beefeater 24 Gin?

The no.24 refers to its 24 hours steeping process of botanicals and the 24-hour lifestyle of England.

211) What does the term 'vapour infusion' on a Bombay Sapphire bottle indicate?

It indicates that the flavour infused in the spirit is by the botanicals coming into contact with the vapours rather than by steeping them in the spirit itself.

212) Which famous Queen's picture could be viewed in the label of a Bombay Sapphire bottle?

The picture of Queen Victoria.

213) What is the colour of Bombay Sapphire Gin bottle?

Sapphire.

214) How many botanicals are used in Bombay Sapphire Gin?

10.

215) Name the rare still used in the production of Bombay Sapphire Gin

Carterhead still.

216) Name India's only London Dry gin (as of April 2021).

Greater Than gin.

217) Give few international brand names of Gin.

Beefeater (London), Gordon's (London), Hendrick's (Scotland), Sipsmith (London) and Tanqueray (London).

218) Give few Indian brand names of Gin

Blue Riband, Greater Than, Jaisalmer, Stranger & Sons, Terai etc.

219) How is gin consumed?

Gin is served with chilled tonic water in tall glassware.

220) Give few mixers for gin.

Tonic water, Carbonated water, Lemon flavoured aerated water etc.

221) What is Vodka?

Vodka is a distilled alcoholic beverage made from grains and potatoes.

222) What is the colour and flavour of vodka?

Vodka is colourless and flavourless. Vodka makers add flavours to vodka to improve its taste and odour.

223) Name two countries that are still in dispute about the origin of vodka.

Russia and Poland.

224) What is the Vodka Belt?

The term refers to countries that focus on large scale production and consumption of vodka. Vodka belt includes countries such as Russia, Poland, Estonia, Latvia, Belarus, Ukraine, Lithuania and majority of the Scandinavian countries.

225) Which are the classic grains used in the production of vodka?

Wheat and rye.

226) What is the meaning of the word 'vodka'?

Vodka means 'little water.'

227) From which Russian word did the term 'vodka' originate?

'Voda.'

228) Which is the material through which vodka is passed as part of its filtration process?

Charcoal.

229) Name the person who discovered that running vodka through activated charcoal removes many of the harsh congeners.

Pyotr Arsenievich Smirnov.

230) What is the nickname given to vodka?

Wife's deceiver (since it has no aroma).

231) Which country consumes the most vodka?

Russia

232) What is Zubrowka vodka?

This vodka is steeped in zubrowka (It is a type of grass on which the European bison or buffalo graze) and comes from Poland. A long blade of the grass floats inside each bottle.

233) Which Russian vodka brand has the nickname 'Stoli'?

Stolichnaya.

234) What is the meaning of the word 'Belvedre'?

'Beautiful to see.'

235) What is the storage period of Vodka?

12 months.

236) Which is the hottest vodka in the world?

250,000 scovilles.

237) Which is the most expensive vodka in the world?

Billionaire Vodka, sells for $3.7m.

238) Where is the museum of Vodka located at?

Russia.

239) Name two gold infused vodka brands.

Smirnoff gold and Royal dragon vodka.

240) Name the vodka brand infused with cognac.

Twenty Grand Gold.

241) Name the vodka brand launched by Donald Trump in 2005.

Trump Vodka.

242) How many times Crystal Head vodka is filtered?

7 times.

243) Which vodka brand is named after its distillery's copper pot still, "Distilleerketel #1?

Ketel One, Netherlands.

244) Name the vodka brand that features the image of the Polish presidential palace in Warsaw on its bottle.

Belvedere, Poland.

245) Which vodka brand claims to be world's first super-premium vodka?

Belvedere, Poland.

246) Where is 'Grey Goose' vodka produced?

France.

247) Name the vodka brand named after the Polish presidential palace in Warsaw (Belweder).

Belvedere, Poland.

248) Name the vodka brand featured in 2015 James bond movie, Spectre.

Belvedere, Poland.

249) Name the vodka brand to feature in maximum Bond movies.

Smirnoff.

250) Which vodka brand's bottle is shaped like a human skull?

Crystal Vodka, Canada.

251) Name the brand of vodka named after the famous composer Frédéric Chopin.

Chopin, Poland.

252) Name the company that owns the famous Smirnoff brand.

Diageo.

253) Which is the Russian version of Smirnoff vodka?

Smirnov vodka.

254) Which vodka brand means Peak and Rock?

Cîroc.

255) Name the vodka brand which is produced around the village of Åhus, Sweden.

Absolut.

256) Is there a flavoured Absolut vodka brand called Absolut Hibiskus?

Yes.

257) Name the first vodka in the world to be made in the 'Maître de Chai' tradition.

Grey Goose.

258) What is the logo of Grey Goose vodka?

Flying French geese.

259) What is the colour of SKYY vodka bottle?

Cobalt blue.

260) Name the vodka brand sold in brushed aluminium bottles.

Danzka, Denmark.

261) Which US vodka is made from wheat and Viognier grapes?

Hangar 1.

262) Name the brand that produces vodka from cow's milk.

Black Cow Vodka, UK.

263) Name the brand which introduced 'Wasabi flavoured vodka' in 2006.

Hangar.

264) Which organic vodka from Kazakhstan is quite popular?

Snow Queen.

265) Name a "bag in a box" vodka brand.

B Square vodka, US.

266) What are the different types of Vodka?

Plain and Flavoured.

267) Give few international brand names of vodka.

Smirnoff (US), Absolut (Sweden), Stolichnaya (Russia), Finlandia (Finland), Hangar 1 (US) and Grey Goose (France).

268) Give few Indian brand names of vodka.

Romanov, Aristocrat, Magic Moments and White Mischief.

269) What is the significance of 'number 21' on a Smirnoff vodka bottle?

It's the recipe number mentioned on Smirnoff vodka bottle.

270) Which are the different flavours of vodka?

Pepper, Chocolate, Apple, Ginger, Cucumber & Mint, Cranberry etc.

271) How vodka could be served?

It could be served as shots, on the rocks and with mixers such as soda, tonic water and lemon flavoured aerated water.

272) What can be served with vodka?

Vodka goes really well with caviar and smoked salmon.

273) Which vodka brand is known as 'Champagne of vodka?'

O2 vodka from England. It is said to be the world's first sparkling vodka.

274) Name bacon infused vodka brand.

Bakon vodka.

275) What is Rum?

Rum is distilled alcoholic beverage made form molasses.

276) What is molasses?

Molasses is a thick, black residue which is the by- product of sugar.

277) Name two other materials from which rum can be obtained.

Fermented sugar cane juice and sugar cane syrup.

278) What are the nick names of Rum?

Barbados water, Demon water, Navy Neaters, Nelson's drink, Pirate's drink, Kill Devil etc.

279) What are the different types of rum?

White/silver, Gold/light, Dark/heavy, Flavoured, Navy and Over proof.

280) What is Navy Rum?

Rum that used to be served to British Naval officers and sailors once is Navy Rum. Its alcohol content is 54.5% ABV.

281) Name the official Navy Rum brand that used to be served on British Navy vessels.

Pusser's Gunpowder Proof rum.

282) What is Over proof Rum?

Rum with high alcoholic content (50-85% ABV).Cruzan 151 and Gosling's 151 are examples.

283) Which brand of rum has the highest alcohol content?

Sunset Very Strong Rum with 84.5% alc./volume.

284) Which is the world's largest rum distillery and where is it located?

Casa Bacardi, Puerto Rico.

285) What is the French and Spanish word for rum?

French-Rhum

Spanish-Ron

286) What does the term 'Añejo' imply on a rum label?

Aged.

287) Who invented Rum?

Slaves.

288) What is the French term used to denote Agricultural Rum?

Rhum Agricole.

289) What is Rhum Agricole?

Rhum manufactured from fresh cane juice.

290) Name the Brazilian rum made from sugarcane juice.

Cachaça.

291) Which is the 'Birthplace of rum'?

Barbados.

292) What is Grog?

A small portion of water and rum.

293) What is White rum?

Rum matured in uncharred oak barrels for one year, filtered and bottled. It has mild flavour and lighter body when compared to other rums.

294) What is Gold rum?

It's medium bodied rum, matured in charred oak barrels for 3 years with the addition of caramel.

295) What is Dark rum?

Rum aged in charred oak barrels above 3 years.

296) Name international brands of rum.

Bacardi (Cuba), Bundaberg (Australia), Captain Morgan (UK), Cruzan (US), Myers's (Jamaica) etc.

297) Name Indian rum brands.

Old Monk, McDowell's, Old Port, Contessa and Hercules.

298) Name few countries that are engaged in rum production.

Barbados, Jamaica, Demerara, Puerto Rico, Cuba, Columbia etc.

299) Rum rations were given to sailors on Royal Navy ships to keep this disease at bay. Which disease am I talking about?

Scurvy.

300) What was the term used to denote 'rum ration'?

Tot.

301) Name the 'Cathedral of rum.'

Bacardi distillery in Cataño, Puerto Rico.

302) What is rum made in the style of Solera system of Sherry called?

Solera rum.

303) Which month is 'U.S National Rum Month'?

August.

304) Which animal is advertised in the Australian rum brand, 'Bundaberg'?

Polar bear.

305) What is the colour of the Bacardi bottle?

Georgia Green.

306) Name the rum brand named after its founder Fred L Myers.

Myers's rum.

307) Which Indian rum brand's name was inspired by the lifestyle of Benedictine monks?

Old Monk.

308) Which company's flavoured rum brand is 'Parrot Bay'?

Captain Morgan.

309) Name a rum brand that pairs well with a Cuban cigar.

Havana Club's Añejo 7 Años.

310) Which Nicaraguan rum brand means "Sugarcane Flower" in Spanish?

Flor de Caña.

311) Which rum brand is named after a mythical giant squid-like sea monster?

Kraken rum.

312) What is the purpose of two loop handles seen on Kraken rum bottle?

For hanging the bottle.

313) Which rum brand takes its name from 'Don Quixote', a Spanish novel.

Don Q.

314) Name few flavours of Bacardi white rum.

Pineapple, Coconut, Tangerine, Grape fruit etc.

315) Name the oldest rum brand in existence.

Mount Gay Rum (from 1793) from Barbados.

316) Which famous rum brand has got 'bat' as its logo?

Bacardi.

317) What does the 'bat' in Bacardi logo signify?

The Bacardi family believes that it's a sign of good luck.

318) Name the only country in the world to have AOC status for its rum production.

Martinique (for its Rum Agricole).

319) After whom Captain Morgan rum is named?

It's named after Sir Henry Morgan, a Welsh born admiral.

320) Which style of Captain Morgan rum is famous?

Spiced rum.

321) Name different spices used in Spiced rum.

Nutmeg, cinnamon, cloves, peppercorns, vanilla bean, orange peel etc.

322) Which is the world's largest selling rum brand (as of July 2020)?

Tanduay from Philippines.

323) Name the Admiral whose nickname was 'Old Grog.'

Admiral Edward Vernon.

324) Mention one of the main reasons that led to the wide popularity of rum during ancient days.

The Triangle trade between New England, Africa and West Indies.

325) Name the first country to produce rum on a commercial basis.

Puerto Rico.

326) From which English word did 'rum' originate?

Rumbullion.

327) Name few mixers for rum.

Cola, lemonade and fruit juices.

328) What is the role of caramel in rum?

Caramel smoothens the blend, gives colour and flavour to the rum.

329) What is Demerara rum?

Demerara rum is a type of rum distilled in Demerara Distillers Limited, British Guyana.

330) Name the first rum distillery in the world.

Mount Gay Distilleries Ltd. of Barbados.

331) What Bermuda, Jamaica, Guatemala, Venezuela and Nicaragua have in common?

These countries have got rum as their national drink.

332) What is Dunder?

Dunder is the residue having yeast of previous batch's fermentation used for commencing the fermentation process of another batch.

333) What is Tequila?

Tequila is a distilled liquor made from the piñas of blue agave tequilana plant.

334) Name North America's first distilled drink.

Tequila.

335) Which country's National drink is Tequila?

Tequila is the National drink of Mexico.

336) Where is Tequila originally produced?

Tequila is originally produced in the city of Tequila, Jalisco state of Mexico.

337) From which word 'tequila' is derived?

The word 'tequila' is said to be of Nahuatl origin and it comes from two words-'Tequitl' (duty, work, job or task) and 'Tlan' (place).

338) What 'Mexican law' says about Tequila?

'Mexican law' says that original tequila is produced only in the Jalisco state of Mexico and in limited areas in the states of Guanajuato, Michoacan, Nayarit and Tamaulipas.

339) Name the ancient civilization associated with tequila.

Aztec.

340) Which is the legally permitted agave plant for producing tequila?

Agave Tequilana Weber Azul.

341) Name two Mexican spirits produced from other agave varieties.

Mezcal and Sotol.

342) Which is the term used to denote the piña harvesters?

Jimador.

343) Name the tool used by the Jimador to harvest piñas.

Coa.

344) Which part of the plant is taken for Tequila making?

Piña.

345) What is the heart of the agave plant?

Piña.

346) Name the traditional stone wheel used to crush cooked piñas.

Tahona.

347) Name the juice obtained after crushing piñas.

Aquameil (honey water).

348) Name the traditional brick oven used for baking agave.

Horno.

349) What is Pulque?

Pulque is the fermented sap of the maguey plant.

350) There are generally 2 categories of Tequila. Name them.

Mixto and 100% Agave.

351) What is Mixto tequila?

The term means 'mixed.' Mixto refers to tequila made from 51% blue agave sugar and 49% non-agave sugars such as cane, corn or a mix of both.

352) What is 100% Agave?

Tequila which is made from 100% blue agave and are bottled in Mexico.

353) Explain different styles of Tequila.

Style	*Meaning*	*Specifications*
Blanco/Silver/Plata	White	0 days-2 months aged.
Joven/Gold/Oro	Young	Mix of Blanco and Reposado tequila.
Reposado/Aged	Rested	2 months–1 year aged.
Añejo	Extra rested	1 year-3 years aged.
Extra Añejo	Ultra rested	Aged for 3 years and above.

354) What are the different types of barrels used for aging tequila?

Oak and used Bourbon barrels.

355) What are Curados?

These are tequilas that are flavoured with fruits.

356) How much percentage of alcohol is present in a 750 ml bottle of Tequila?

The alcoholic content could vary between 38 to 55%.

357) When is 'U.S National Tequila Day' celebrated?

'U.S National Tequila Day' is celebrated every year on 24th of July.

358) How is Tequila consumed?

The Mexicans prefer it neat. Consuming tequila in the form of 'shots' along with salt and a wedge of lemon is also common. The salt licked first will bring down the harshness of tequila which is gulped down and the lemon wedge sucked enhances the experience. Tequila could be taken in the form of cocktails-Seltzer water, grape fruit soda, orange juice etc. are popular mixers.

359) Which is the most famous tequila based cocktail in the world?

Margarita.

360) Name the first commercial producer of Tequila in Mexico.

Jose Cuervo.

361) Who was the first to introduce Tequila in United States?

Don Cenobio Sauza, the founder of tequila brand Sauza was the first to introduce Tequila in United States.

362) Name the Tequila brand that comes with a glass Tiki inside the bottle

Voodoo Tiki Tequila.

363) Give few examples for Curados (flavoured/infused Tequila).

Voodoo Tiki Tequila Desert Rose (pear), Voodoo Tiki Tequila Green Dragon (lime), Voodoo Tiki Tequila Blue Dragon (kiwi) etc.

364) What is Mezcal?

Mezcal is a distilled alcoholic beverage produced from agave plant.

365) Differentiate Mezcal from Tequila.

Criteria of differentiation	Mezcal	Tequila
Area of production	Can be produced in 8 regions of Mexico	Can be produced in 5 regions of Mexico
Main area of production	Oaxaca	State of Jalisco
Agave variety	Produced from more than 30 different varieties of agave	Made only from Agave Tequilana Weber Azul
Cooking of piñas	In earthen pits	In brick/industrial ovens
Distillation	In clay/pot stills	In copper pot stills

366) What is 'Vodquila'?

Vodquila is a brand of tequila produced by blending six times distilled vodka with tequila.

367) What is 'Rumquila'?

It's a brand of tequila produced by blending dark rum and tequila.

368) 'All tequilas are mescals but not all mescals are tequilas.' Explain the statement.

All tequilas are made from the piñas of a specific agave plant (Agave Tequilana Weber Azul) whereas mescal could be produced from more than 30 different varieties of agave.

369) Mention five brand names of tequila.

Jose Cuervo, Sauza, Patrón, Pepe Lopez and Montezuma.

370) Name the tequila brand owned by the popular Hollywood actor, Dwayne 'The Rock' Johnson.

Teremana.

371) Is it true that Tequila needs to be sipped slowly rather than consuming it in one shot?

Yes, Tequila needs to be sipped slowly.

372) Name the tequila brand that has the image of Olmec head.

Olmeca.

373) What is Sotol?

Sotol is a distilled alcoholic beverage made from piña of the Dasylirion wheeleri plant that comes from the northern region of Mexico particularly from Chihuahua region.

374) What is Bacanora?

Bacanora is a Mexican liquor that hails from Sonora and is made from Agave angustifolia haw plant.

375) What is Raicilla?

It's a single distilled liquor from the Jalisco State of Mexico. Raicilla is produced from agave plants and tends to fruitier and slightly stronger in taste than its counterpart, tequila.

376) Which is the National drink of China?

Baijiu.

377) What is Baijiu?

A colourless Chinese liquor made from fermented grains (primarily sorghum) is Baijiu.

378) What was Baijiu originally known as?

Shaojiu meaning 'burnt wine.'

379) Name the world's first bar set exclusively for Baijiu.

Capital Spirits bar located in Beijing.

380) Which are the main four categories of Baijiu?

Baijiu is mainly categorized on the basis of its aroma-Strong aroma, Sauce aroma, Light aroma and Rice aroma.

381) What is the nick name given to Baijiu?

Sorghum spirit.

382) Name a popular brand of Baijiu.

Ming River.

383) Which is the largest selling liquor in the world?

Soju.

384) What is Soju?

Soju is a colourless liquor often referred as 'Korean vodka' made from rice and other grains.

385) What is Shochu?

Shochu is a Japanese distilled alcoholic beverage made from grains and vegetables.

386) What is the main difference between Soju and Shochu?

Soju is produced in Korea and Shochu in Japan.

387) Which liquor has the nick name Lion's Milk?

Raki.

388) What is the nick name given to Absinthe?

The Green Fairy (la fée verte).

389) What is the traditional colour of Absinthe?

Green.

390) What do you mean by 'louche' of Absinthe?

Absinthe turns to 'milky white' and becomes cloudy when water is added to it.

391) What is 'holy trinity 'of Absinthe?

The combination of Grand wormwood, aniseed and fennel.

392) Which plant is referred to as 'Absinthe plant'?

The 'wormwood' plant.

393) Name the liquor which is served in kanoakia glassware.

Ouzo.

394) What is Ouzo?

It's a distilled alcoholic beverage with aniseed flavour, made from the remainings of grape must.

395) Name two countries that produce Ouzo.

Cyprus and Greece.

396) What is Vinjak?

Vinjak is a dark Siberian brandy served as a digestif.

397) Name the first alcoholic beverage to be consumed in outer space.

Metaxa, grape brandy from Greece.

398) What is Feni/Fenny?

Feni/Fenny is a transparent distilled alcoholic beverage made from cashew apples and coconut.

399) Which country holds GI (Geographical Indication) for Cashew Feni?

India.

400) Name the Indian state which primarily produces Feni.

Goa.

401) In which year did India received the 'GI' status for Feni?

2009.

402) How many times Feni is distilled?

Thrice.

403) How traditionally Feni is served?

Traditionally, Feni is served in a coconut shell.

404) Name the traditional still used for Feni.

Bhatti.

405) How Feni could be consumed?

Straight, On the rocks, Feni with Limca etc.

406) Give few brand names of Feni.

Lembranca, Cazulo, Big Boss, Treasure Island, Fish & Feni, PVV, Serenade etc.

5.6 Tea, Coffee & Energy Drinks

1) What is Tea?

Tea is a stimulating beverage produced by steeping tea dust/tea leaves in boiling water.

2) Name the tropical evergreen bush from which the leaves are collected for making tea dust.

Camellia sinensis.

3) Where was tea first discovered?

China.

4) Who is said to have discovered tea leaves?

Shen Nung, a Chinese emperor.

5) Name the world's largest tea producing country.

China.

6) What are the popular teas produced in India?

Assam, Darjeeling and Nilgiri.

7) Which are the leading tea producing countries?

China, India, Kenya, Srilanka and Japan.

8) What are the different ways of packing tea?

Leaf tea, tea bags, envelopes, instant and pods.

9) Which is the most popular type of tea in China?

Green tea.

10) Name few varieties of Chinese teas.

Jin fo, Keemun and Lapsang Souchong.

11) What are the different types of tea?

Black tea, green tea, oolong tea, puerh tea, white tea, yellow tea and flavoured tea.

12) What is Black Tea?

Black tea is a dark coloured tea with strong aroma and flavor made from oxidized tea leaves. The manufacturing process of this tea varies from country to country but mostly it's either Orthodox or CTC (Cut, Tear and Curl). Twinings and Davids Tea are black tea brands.

13) Which tea is known as 'Red tea' in China?

Black tea.

14) What is Oolong Tea?

Oolong Tea is a semi-fermented or semi-oxidised tea that originated in the Fujian province of China. It has light delicate flavor. Twinings is a brand of oolong tea.

15) What is Green Tea?

Green Tea is unfermented or unoxidised tea that possesses pungent flavour. The name comes from its emerald green colour and is said to have many medicinal properties.

16) Give three benefits of green tea.

Consumption of green tea might help in weight loss, may improve functioning of brain and lower the risk of cancer in humans.

17) What are the principles of Japanese tea ceremony?

Wa (harmony), Kei (respect), Sei (purity) and Jaku (serenity).

18) Name the green tea powder used in Japanese tea ceremony.

Matcha.

19) What is the colour of green tea after brewing?

Straw or pale yellow colour.

20) Why green tea has more health benefits than black tea?

Green tea has good amount of anti-oxidants in it. The higher proportion of flavonoids particularly catechins and epigallocatechin gallate makes it unique.

21) Name the widely consumed and most famous Japanese green tea.

Sencha.

22) What is Flavoured tea?

A tea to which flavourings (natural or artificial) are added is termed as Flavoured tea. An example is Earl Grey tea (Black tea to which oil of bergamot is added).

23) What is Puerh tea or pu'er tea?

Puerh tea is a type of fermented tea that comes from the Yunnan province of China.

24) What is White Tea?

White tea is an expensive tea prepared from the buds of a variant of the tea plant that grows high up on Chinese mountains. The tiny silver hairs that cover the buds give tea a white appearance. Twinings and Taylors are popular white tea brands.

25) In which province of China is white tea generally grown?

In the Fujian province.

26) Why is white tea expensive?

The tea is expensive as its buds and leaves are manually harvested once a year.

27) What is Yellow tea?

A type of tea from China which is bright yellow in colour with a delicate fruit flavour is Yellow tea. The colour is gained by a process called 'Sealed Yellowing.'

28) How many minutes the tea should be left for fresh brewing to get maximum benefits of its antioxidants?

Around 3 to 5 minutes.

29) What is Kombucha?

Kombucha is a fermented tea preparation made with bacteria, sugar, yeast and tea.

30) What is Blue tea/Butterfly pea tea?

It's a kind of herbal tea native to South East Asia which is produced by infusing flowers and leaves of Clitoria ternatea plant along with dried lemon grass.

31) What are the different grades of Black tea?

FOP-Flowery Orange Pekoe

OP-Orange Pekoe

P-Pekoe

FP-Flowery Pekoe

BOP-Broken Orange Pekoe.

32) What are Tisanes?

Tisanes are flavoured and herbal teas consumed for medicinal benefits.

Camomile, Mint, Rosehip, Peppermint (All are Herbal teas)

Cherry, Lemon, Blackcurrant (All are Fruit teas).

33) Which tea is known as the 'Champagnes of Teas'?

Darjeeling tea.

34) Why Darjeeling tea is referred to as 'Champagnes of Teas'?

It has got Geographical Indication status and hence Darjeeling tea should be only grown in Darjeeling and are not grown elsewhere.

35) Which grape's flavor can be felt while sipping a cup of Darjeeling tea?

Muscatel.

36) Name the most expensive tea in the world.

Da Hong Pao from China.

37) What makes Da Hong Pao world's most expensive tea?

The tea leaves used in its preparation are collected from tea plants growing in Wuyi Mountains for more than 300 years.

38) What is Panda Dung tea?

Panda Dung tea is a tea made from tea leaves which were fertilized using the dung of panda bears.

39) What are the differences between Assam tea and Darjeeling tea?

Criteria of differentiation	Assam tea	Darjeeling tea
Popularity	Less popular	More popular than Assam tea
Taste	Less spicier	Spicier than Assam tea
Best way to consume	With milk	Without milk

40) What is Nilgiri tea?

A type of tea that hails from the Nilgiris district of Tamil Nadu, South India is Nilgiri tea.

41) What is Keemun?

Keemun is a popular black tea variety from Qimen County of Anhui Province, China.

42) What is Tippy tea?

Tea with greater portions of tips is used to prepare caffeine rich tea called Tippy tea.

43) How much tea is there in a tea bag?

Approximately 1.5 to 2 grams.

44) What is Hibiscus tea?

Hibiscus tea is a style of tea prepared with the petals of hibiscus flower.

45) Name few of the popular Indian tea preparations.

Adrak chai, Kesar chai, Elachi ki chai, Masala chai and Tandoori chai.

46) What is Tandoori chai?

Small clay bowls (kulhars) are put in tandoor, removed and half brewed tea (blended tea leaves and aromatic spices) is added into the hot empty bowls. It was invented by Amol Dilip Rajdeo.

47) What is Samovar?

A traditional Kashmiri kettle made either of copper or metal that holds charcoal in the centre, enabling to brew and boil tea.

48) Name three stimulants present in tea.

Caffeine, Theobromine and Theophylline.

49) Which chemical compound is responsible for the bitter taste in tea?

Tannin.

50) What are Fannings?

Fannings are broken tea leaves of lower grade quality.

51) Name the tea which is billed as the world's most refined tea.

Lip tea.

52) What is Lip tea?

Lip Tea is Chinese tea leaves of which are picked by virgins using their lips.

53) Why Virgin White Tea is named so?

The name is given as the tea leaves are untouched and are harvested using scissors.

54) Which is the most popular historical event related to tea?

Boston Tea Party.

55) Name two equipment used in tea making.

Plunger and Tea ball.

56) Which is the most consumed beverage in the world?

Tea.

57) What is Coffee?

Coffee is a stimulating beverage produced by grinding coffee beans obtained from a tropical evergreen shrub.

58) Name the main stimulant present in coffee.

Caffeine.

59) Name two popular varieties of coffee beans.

Coffee Arabica and coffee robusta.

60) Which is the traditional copper coffee pot with a long handle used in the preparation of Turkish coffee?

Cezve/Ibrik.

61) What is Civet/Luwark coffee?

Civet coffee, popularly known as Kopi luwak is the world's most expensive coffee made from coffee beans taken from the 'poops' of civet cat.

62) What is Espresso?

An Italian dark, black coffee preparation made by passing steam with high pressure through coffee powder.

63) What is Single Shot Espresso?

A Single Shot Espresso refers to 30 ml of espresso.

64) What is Doppio Espresso?

A dark, black coffee preparation with double amount of coffee powder than the normal. It's generally 60 ml.

65) What is Café Latte?

Espresso coffee brewed in milk served with or without foam.

66) What is Espresso Americano?

Black coffee preparation with espresso and hot water.

67) What is Espresso Ristretto?

Espresso Ristretto refers to concentrated espresso coffee preparation prepared by switching off the espresso machine towards the end of coffee making process.

68) What is Caffè Mocha/Mocaccino?

Caffè Mocha is a coffee preparation with espresso, milk and chocolate syrup. It is named after the City of Mocha located in Yemen.

69) Give few examples for speciality coffee preparations.

Irish coffee (Irish whiskey), Highland coffee (Scotch whisky), Calypso coffee (Tia Maria) and Russian coffee (Vodka).

70) What are coffee pods/capsules?

Coffee pods/capsules refer to pre-ground coffee that comes in pod/capsule form used in an espresso machine for preparing an individual portion of coffee. Nespresso and Vero are renowned brands of coffee pods.

71) What is the role of chicory in South Indian coffee preparations?

Chicory adds flavour and gives body to South Indian coffee.

72) Why Filter Coffee is named so?

The name comes from the metal filter used to brew the coffee.

73) What is Turkish coffee?

Turkish coffee is an unfiltered, ground black coffee prepared in a small copper pot (cezve) over fire. Sugar is added while brewing it and the coffee is served with foam. A glass of water and Turkish Delight is generally offered along with the coffee.

74) What is Cappuccino?

Cappuccino is a hot coffee drink that features black coffee, milk froth and cinnamon stick. The name comes from the colour of Capuchin robe of friars that resembles the colour of coffee.

75) Give four brand names of coffee.

Brazilian Santos, Colombia Armenia, Costa Rica San Marco Tarrazu and Ethiopian Harrar Longberry.

76) What are Energy drinks?

Energy drinks are soft drinks that will boost the energy of a consumer.

77) Name few constituents of energy drink.

Vitamins, Essential salts like Sodium and Potassium, Vital nutrients

78) Give few examples for energy drink brands.

Red Bull, Cloud 9, Restless, Burn and Tsinga.

79) Name an energy sports drink.

Gatrode.

80) Name one energy drink from the Coca Cola Company.

Burn.

5.7 Water

1) What is potable water?

Water which is of drinking quality, accepted by human body is potable water.

2) What should be done to make water 'potable'?

Water should either be available from natural sources such as springs or should be treated to remove impurities and pollutants.

3) Give the role of water in human body.

Digestion, removes toxins, aids in absorption of food, maintains body temperature etc.

4) Is water a beverage?

No, water is generally not considered as a drink or beverage.

5) What is bottled water?

Bottled water is water filled and sealed in safe bottles that are meant for human consumption.

6) Classify bottled water.

Still, aerated, natural spring and mineral water.

7) What is bottled still water?

It is bottled water that lacks aeration and is generally used to replace tap water.

8) What is aerated/sparkling/carbonated water?

These are carbon dioxide infused water and are classified into three-plain aerated water, flavoured aerated water and special aerated water.

9) What is plain aerated water?

Plain aerated water is water without essences or flavours in it. Example is soda.

10) What is seltzer water?

Seltzer water is plain aerated water.

11) Differentiate soda from club soda.

Criteria of differentiation	Soda	Club soda
Addition of carbon dioxide	Natural and artificial	Artificial
Mineral content	No	Yes
Taste	Plain	Presence of minerals might generate salt flavour

12) New two minerals that is present in club soda.

Disodium phosphate and potassium sulfate.

13) Why is club soda named so?

It's named after Kildare Street Club located in Dublin that commissioned the original trademarked club soda.

14) What is flavoured aerated water?

Aerated water to which essences or flavours are added to impart taste and flavour.

15) Give examples for flavoured aerated water.

Coca-Cola (cola), Sprite (lemon), Mirinda (orange) and Limca (lemon and lime).

16) What is special aerated water?

Special aerated water is a type of aerated water with flavour and unique properties. Examples are Tonic water and Ginger ale.

17) What is Tonic water?

Tonic water is quinine flavoured aerated water that has got medicinal properties. It is consumed as a medicine to fight against malaria and stomach infections.

18) What is Ginger ale?

Ginger ale is sweetened, ginger flavoured aerated water.

19) What is Root beer?

Root beer is a caffeine free, non-alcoholic aerated drink. The word 'root' refers to the root of sassafras tree that gives the beer its predominant flavour. A&W is a famous brand of root beer.

20) What is spring water?

Water which is directly bottled from natural springs is termed as spring water. This kind of water is said to have minerals naturally present in it and the amount of minerals vary according to its source of origin.

21) Give four brand names of spring water with its country of origin.

Brand name	*Character*	*Country of origin*
Ashbourne	Still/Carbonated	England
Highland spring	Still/Carbonated	Scotland
Malvern	Still/Carbonated	England
Strathmore	Sparkling	Scotland

22) What is mineral water?

Mineral water is water with different levels of dissolved minerals and trace elements. It could be natural or artificial. The amount of minerals present is mentioned as TDS (Total Dissolved Solids) in the bottle. The regulation of FDA is that the quantity of dissolved solids present in mineral water should be minimum of 250 parts per million from the source where it is bottled.

23) What are the main styles of mineral water?

Still and sparkling.

24) Give five brand names of mineral water with its country of origin.

Brand name	*Character*	*Country of origin*
Badoit	Semi-sparkling	France
Buxton	Still/Carbonated	England
Evian	Still	France
Perrier	Sparkling	France
San Pellegrino	Carbonated	Italy

25) Name India's first sparkling natural mineral water brand.

Boca from Himachal Pradesh.

26) What are the different types of mineral water?

Alkaline, Aperient, Chalybeate, Lithiated and Sulphurous water.

27) Why many people prefer bottled water to tap water?

Bottled water is easy to carry, lacks chemicals like chlorine and is made under strict safety standards.

28) What is the expiry date of bottled mineral water?

Though the water doesn't have any expiry date, the bottle has. Hence, it's better not to drink water from plastic bottles if they are more than 6 months old.

29) Why bottled mineral water comes with an expiry date?

The bottle could create problem for the water filled in it after a certain point of time. It might contaminate the water with chemicals.

30) How will you serve mineral and spring water?

Mineral and spring water is served either in water goblet or Paris goblet from the right hand side of the guest. The bottle is kept on the left hand side of the guest for refilling purpose.

The crown or the cap and seal should be removed in front of the guest.

31) Who created the first artificial mineral water?

It was created by an English scientist, Dr. William Brownrigg in the year 1741.

32) Who invented Perrier, the famous mineral water brand?

A French doctor named Louis Perrier.

33) Name the mineral water brand recommended by James Bond in Ian Fleming's 1960 novel, 'For Your Eyes Only.'

Perrier.

34) Name the mineral water brand known as 'The Champagne of Table Waters.'

Perrier from France.

35) Name the 'Queen of Table Waters.'

Appollinaris from Germany.

36) Which mineral water brand has red triangle symbol?

Appollinaris.

37) Name the French bottled water that features three mountains as its logo.

Evian.

38) When water becomes 'potable'?

When water is free from microorganisms, chemicals and other pollutants it becomes potable.

39) Which is the bottled water brand best identified by its distinctive green coloured bottle?

Perrier from France.

40) Which is the largest bottled brand in the world?

As per 2020, Aquafina of PepsiCo is the largest bottled brand in the world.

5.8 Wine

1) What is Wine?

Wine is an alcoholic beverage obtained from fermented grape juice that has been carried through in the district of its origin and according to local traditions, practices and law.

2) What is Mead?

Answer- Mead is a fermented alcoholic beverage made from honey and water.

3) Name two Gods of wine.

Answer- Dionysus and Bacchus.

4) Give the Latin word from which the English term 'wine' is derived.

Vinum.

5) What is 'Mei'?

An ancient Persian wine.

6) Name the ancient Greek 'God of wine.'

Dionysus.

7) Name the ancient Roman 'God of wine.'

Bacchus.

8) What is Shedeh?

An ancient drink of Egypt made from grapes.

9) Name the jar used by the ancient Greeks and Romans to store wine.

Amphora.

10) What is 'Amphora'?

Amphorae were air tight containers that were made of clay.

11) Name the Father of modern wine bottle.

Sir Kenelm Digby.

12) Name the oldest and most productive cork tree in the world.

Whistler Tree in Portugal.

13) Name the process of converting grape juice into wine.

Fermentation.

14) What is the science of wine making called?

Oenology.

15) Though wines could be made from any kind of fruits, why 'grape' still remains as the base of many wines?

Grape has the right amount of sugar and acidic level needed for making wines. Since, these elements are naturally present in it many wine makers produce wine from grapes.

16) Differentiate wine grape from table grape.

Criteria of differentiation	*Wine grape*	*Table grape*
Size of grape	Small	Big
Sugar level	Higher than table grape	Low
Acidic level	Higher than table grape	Low
Brix level	24-26	17-19
Skin	Thicker	Thinner

17) What are the different parts of a grape?

Stalk, Skin, Pips and Pulp.

18) Name the whitish cloudy coat seen on the skin of grape.

Bloom.

19) What is Bloom?

Bloom is a waxy substance which holds wild yeasts and wine yeasts along with millions of minute enzymes.

20) Name the colouring pigment present on the skin of red grape.

Anthocyanin.

21) Name the colouring pigment present on the skin of white grape.

Flavones.

22) What is Tannin?

Tannin is a compound which is present in grape and is bitter in flavor. It acts as a preservative and antioxidant.

23) Which part/parts of the grape has tannin/tannic acid?

Stalk and Pips.

24) Give few examples for wine producing vine species.

Vitis vinifera, Vitis riparia, Vitis rupestris, Vitis labrusca etc.

25) Why grapes belonging to Vitis vinifera family are used in making wine?

Grapes belonging to Vitis vinifera family have higher sugar content responsible for producing quality wines.

26) Give few examples for red/black grape varieties.

Cabernet Sauvignon, Pinot Noir, Gamay, Barbera, Merlot etc.

27) Give few examples for green/white grape varieties.

Chardonnay, Riesling, Muscat, Chenin Blanc, Sauvignon Blanc etc.

28) Name the grape variety which is popularly known as 'King of Red wines.'

Cabernet Sauvignon.

29) Which white grape variety is known as 'King of White wines'?

Chardonnay.

30) Name the grape variety known as 'Steen' in South Africa.

Chenin blanc.

31) Which red grape varietal is known as 'Shiraz' in Australia?

Syrah.

32) Name the grape varietal which is also known as Prosecco.

Glera.

33) How many grape varietals are legally permitted to be used in the production of Champagne? Name them.

Seven. The grapes are Chardonnay, Pinot Noir, Pinot Meunier, Arbane, Pinot gris, Petit Meslier and Pinot blanc.

34) Name the primary grape varieties used in the making of Champagne.

Chardonnay (white), Pinot Noir (black) and Pinot Meunier (black).

35) Which are the three grape varieties involved in the production of Cava?

Macabeo, Parellada and Xarel-lo.

36) Name the grape varieties used in the making of Sherry

Palomino (white), Pedro Ximénez (white) and Moscatel (white).

37) Name the grape varieties used in the making of Port.

Almost 60 grape varieties are available for making Port. But these days, the Port producers have limited it to 5 grape varieties. They are Touriga Nacional, Touriga Franca/Francesa, Tinta Roriz, Tinta Cão and Tinta Barroca, all being red grape varietals. Codega, Malvasia and Rabigato are the white varietals used.

38) What is Viticulture?

Viticulture denotes all the processes that are included in the cultivation of vines.

39) Give few steps of viticulture.

Ploughing, Pruning, Grafting, Weed control, Vine training etc.

40) Why is ploughing done for the soil before planting vines?

Ploughing is done with the purpose of aerating the soil.

41) What is Pruning?

Pruning is removal of unwanted parts of the vine.

42) Why pruning is done for the vines?

It is done to regulate the yield thereby increasing the quality of the crop.

43) Name few vine diseases

Botrytis Cinerea, Phomopsis, Phylloxera, Pierce's Disease etc.

44) What is Phylloxera?

Phylloxera is a kind of vine disease. It is a small yellow insect that punctures the roots of the vine and form galls on the underside of the leaves.

45) What is Phomopsis/Dead arm?

It's a type of vine disease caused by a fungus called Phomopsis viticola. Phomopsis is identified by the appearance of black cracks at the base of the shoot which will finally break off.

46) What is Botrytis Cinerea/Grey Rot?

Botrytis Cinerea is a type of fungus which can be either benevolent or malevolent. When it is benevolent, it increases the sweetness of the grape whereas in the malevolent form it destroys colour pigmentation of the grape and gives an unpleasant taste to the wine.

47) What is Noble rot/Pourriture noble/Muffa nobile/Edelfäule?

It's a condition in which the Botrytis Cinerea fungus will act on grape by removing the water, making the grapes to shrivel thereby increasing its sugar content.

48) Name few grape varieties that are affected by Noble rot.

Chenin blanc, Sémillon, Sauvignon blanc, Muscadelle, Furmint, Gewürztraminer etc.

49) Give the names of few countries and its regions where sweet wines are produced from botrytised affected grapes.

Country	*Region/Wine style*
France	Sauternes
Italy	Orvieto
Germany	Beerenauslese & Trocken beerenauslese
Hungary	Tokaj
Australia	Riverina

50) Classify wines.

Wines are classified into Table, Sparkling, Fortified and Aromatised wines.

51) Classify Table wines

Red wine, White wine and Rosé wine.

52) What are Table/Still/Dinner/Natural wines (Vin ordinaire)?

Table wines are those wines that are served on the table and makes up the largest category of wines. The main purpose of these wines is to accompany the food or meal.

53) What is Vinification?

All the operations done to transform the juice from the freshly crushed grapes into an acceptable standard of wine is called as Vinification.

54) Name few factors which affect the quality of wine (factors affecting wine production).

Location, Soil, Climate, Type of vine and grape used, Skill of the wine maker etc.

55) What are Red wines?

Red wine is a type of table wine made from red (black) grapes and is more full bodied than white and rosé wines. They are often complex and robust than white wines.

56) How red wine gets its colour?

The skin of the red grape variety is allowed to rest with the 'must' so that the desired colour is obtained.

57) Give two examples for red wines.

Ruffino Chianti from Italy and Château Latour from France.

58) What are White wines?

White wine is a kind of table wine which could be made from both black and white grapes. The flavour varies from extreme dry to extremely sweet and the colour from pale straw to deep gold.

59) How white wine gets its colour?

The skin of the grape variety is allowed to rest with the 'must' for a very short duration of time so that the desired colour is obtained.

60) Give two classic examples for white wines.

Château Cheval Blanc and Château d'Yquem of France.

61) What are Rosé/Pink wines?

Rosé/Pink wine is a kind of table wine which is made from black grapes. It can also be made by mixing red and white wine to the desired colour. Rosé/Pink wine is slightly sweeter and fruity when compared with red and white wines.

62) What is Blush wine?

Blush wine is the term commonly used in USA to denote Rosé wines made entirely from red grapes.

63) Give two examples for Rosé wines.

Mateus Rosé and Sula Blush Zinfandel 2011 are examples for Rosé wines.

64) Give five examples for wine equipment.

Wine chiller, wine decanter, wine glasses, waiter's friend, wine bucket etc.

65) What is Corkscrew?

Corkscrew is a wine equipment used by a waiter to pull out the cork from the wine bottle. It consists of 2 parts-a wooden handle and a worm (spiral metallic part).

66) What is Angel corkscrew?

Angel corkscrew is an extended version of corkscrew that features 2 levers, one on each side. It has a worm in the centre and when inserted into the cork and rotated, the levers on both the sides raises up

67) What is Waiter's friend?

The most commonly used wine opener by the waiters is a Waiter's friend. It is also known as Sommelier knife and consists of 4 parts-handle, retractable knife, worm and fulcrum.

68) Why a wine basket/cradle is preferred during the decanting process?

If the wine contains sediments it is rested on the wine basket/cradle for certain time so that the sediments fall to one side of the bottle. Hence few prefer this equipment during the decanting process.

69) What is Ah-so?

Ah-so is a wine equipment used to extract cork from a wine bottle without puncturing the cork. The two prongs (one long and the other short) are inserted through the sides of the cork and it is pulled out.

70) What is Tastevin/ Sommelier's Cup?

Tastevin sometimes referred as Sommelier's Cup is a tool of Sommelier and is normally hung around his neck. It is a shallow cup or saucer made from silver or glass or porcelain and is used by the Sommelier to check the taste and colour of the wine.

71) What are Sparkling/Bubbly wines?

Sparkling wines are wines that have carbon dioxide present in it.

72) Give a list of sparkling wines hailing from different countries

Wine	Country
Champagne	France
Cava	Spain
Qualitätschaumwein/Sekt	Germany
Espumante	Portugal
Asti-spumante & Prosecco	Italy
Cuvee Napa	United States
Cap Classique	South Africa
Sparkling Shiraz	Australia

73) Name the most popular sparkling wine in the world.

Champagne from France.

74) What was Champagne originally called in its initial days?

Vins du diable/Devil's Wine/Cork-jumper/Petillant.

75) Name the 'undisputed king of all sparkling wines.'

Champagne.

76) Which method is followed in Champagne making?

Méthode Champenoise.

77) Name the sparkling wine which is widely used in the world for toasting/celebration purposes.

Champagne.

78) Which sparkling wine is of highest choice for christening ships?

Champagne.

79) Name the sparkling wine which is known as 'King of Bubbles.'

Champagne.

80) Name any four different ways by which sparkle (CO2) could be added to still wine.

Méthode Champenoise, Méthode Cuve close, Méthode Transvasage and Méthode Gazifie.

81) What is Méthode Champenoise/ Champagne method/ Méthode Traditionnelle/Método Classico?

It's one of the ways by which carbon dioxide is infused to the wine. Fermented wine is made to ferment for second time in the bottle by the addition of sugar and yeast. The resulting carbon dioxide is trapped inside. Sparkling wines made through this process tend to be costly since it requires special bottles and corks.

82) What is Méthode Cuve close/Charmat process/Bulk method/ Closed tank method?

It's one of the ways by which carbon dioxide is infused to the wine. Wine undergoes secondary fermentation in a sealed tank and then is filtered and finally bottled under pressure.

83) What is Méthode Transvasage?

It's one of the ways by which carbon dioxide is infused to the wine. The secondary fermentation takes place inside the bottle (like the Traditional method).The wine is then chilled and disgorged into a pressurized tank. There the wine is filtered and then bottled under pressure.

84) What is Méthode Gazifie?

It's one of the ways by which carbon dioxide is infused to the wine. The carbon dioxide is pumped into the chilled wine under pressure.

85) What is 'Assemblage'?

Assemblage is the art of blending Champagne.

86) What is 'liqueur de tirage'?

A mix of old champagne, sugar and yeast.

87) What is 'liqueur d' expedition'/'dosage'?

A solution of cane sugar and older champagne.

88) What is Remuage/Riddling?

Remuage, also known as Riddling is a traditional method (manually done) employed to clear the sediments present in Champagne.

89) What is Gyropalette?

The mechanical way of doing manual Remuage/Riddling is Gyropalette.

90) Who is a Remueur?

Remueur is a person who is an expert in Riddling process.

91) What is Pupitre?

A pupitre, also known as riddling rack consists of a pair of heavy hinged rectangular boards to form an inverted V shape. Each board contains 60 holes and holds the champagne bottle at 45° angle. It is used to clear the sediments present in Champagne.

92) Who designed Pupitre?

Madame Veuve Clicquot.

93) What is Dégorgement (Disgorging)?

The process of removing sediments (in the frozen form) from the Champagne bottle is termed as Dégorgement (Disgorging).

94) What is Agrafe?

Agrafe is the metallic clip used to fix the temporary caps on a Champagne bottle once.

95) What is Muselet/Wire cage/Muzzle?

Muselet/Wire cage/Muzzle refers to the metallic cage used to affix the cork of Champagne bottle in place.

96) What is Plaque de Muselet?

The metallic plate seen on top of the Champagne cork is known as Plaque de Muselet.

97) Who is a Placomusophile?

A person who collects Plaque de Muselet of different Champagne brands is termed as Placomusophile.

98) From which Latin word is Champagne derived from?

'Campania' meaning open, flat land/country side.

99) Name the most expensive style of Champagne.

Cuvée de prestige/Luxury Cuvée also known as Prestige Cuvée.

100) What is Cuvée de prestige?

This style of Champagne is commonly known as Luxury Cuvée or Prestige Cuvée and are mostly used for grand occasions. These are fabulous expensive wines made in the best years and are regarded as the best product of a particular Champagne house.

101) Give two famous examples for Cuvée de prestige Champagne brands.

Moët & Chandon's Dom Pérignon and Pol Roger's Cuvée Sir Winston Churchill.

102) What is Vintage Champagne?

These are well matured Champagne wines that are made from grapes of a single good year. It is normally aged on the lees for at least three years.

103) What is Non-Vintage Champagne?

Non-vintage Champagne is a blend of wines from different years.

104) What is 'Blanc de Blancs' Champagne?

A French term that literally means "white of white". White champagne made from white grapes. This term is used to designate champagnes made only from Chardonnay grapes.

105) What is 'Blanc de Noirs' Champagne?

A French term that literally means "white of blacks". White champagne entirely made from black grapes. Pinot Noir, Pinot Meunier or a blend of the two is used for the champagne making.

106) What is Pink/Rosé Champagne?

This style of Champagne could be of vintage or non-vintage character. Wine makers mix red wine (Pinot Noir) and white wine to create this wonder. Another way is using the saignée technique following a short maceration. i.e., by leaving the black grape skins with the juice until it becomes pink in colour.

107) Which Champagne house was the first to manufacture Rosé Champagne commercially?

Ruinart (1764).

108) What is Crémant?

Crémant is the generic French name for semi-sparkling wine made in that country outside the region of Champagne having pressure of about 3 ½ atmosphere.

109) What is Brut Champagne?

The word 'Brut' on a Champagne wine label implies that the wine is dry (1% sugar).

It contains less than 15 g/l of residual sugar.

110) Which is the most common style of Champagne produced in the world?

Brut.

111) Who was the first to make 'Brut' (dry) Champagne?

Madame Louise Pommery (1874).

112) What is the difference between 'Brut Sans Année' and 'Brut Millésimé'?

'Brut Sans Année' refers to dry Champagne made with wines of different years whereas 'Brut Millésimé' refers to dry Champagne of a particular year.

113) Which is the driest Champagne of all?

Brut zero/Au Sauvage.

114) Give the size of various Champagne bottles.

Name of the bottle	*Equivalent size*	*Capacity in litres*
Melchisedech	40 bottles	30 litres
Primat/Goliath	36 bottles	27 litres
Sovereign	35 bottles	26.25 litres
Solomon	24 bottles	18 litres
Nebuchadnezzar	20 bottles	15 litres
Balthazar	16 bottles	12 litres
Salmanazar	12 bottles	9 litres
Methuselah/Methusalem/Imperial	8 bottles	6 litres
Rehoboam	6 bottles	4.5 litres
Jeroboam/Double magnum	4 bottles	3 litres
Magnum	2 bottles	1.5 litres
Bottle	1 bottle	.75 litres
Half bottle/Demi	½ bottle	.375 litres
Quarter/Split	¼ bottle	.1875 litres

115) What is Aspersion?

Aspersion is a term related to the vineyards in Champagne region of France and is a method of preventing frost from forming on the vines and grapes.

116) Name the only European wine region where it is permitted to mix red and white wines to create rosé wines.

Champagne.

117) Name the Champagne districts.

Montagne de Reims (Mountain of Reims), Côte des Blancs (Coast of the white/Great white hill side), Vallée de la Marne (Valley of the Marne), Vignoble de l'aube (Vineyards of Aube) and Côte des Sézanne (Coast of Sézanne).

118) What kind of soil is seen in the Champagne region?

Chalky soil.

119) What is Belemnita quadrata?

Belemnita quadrata is the chalky subsoil seen in Champagne region of France which consists of the fossils of belemnite mollusk.

120) In which year was Champagne region of France declared as a UNESCO Heritage Site?

In the year 2015.

121) What is CIVC?

The regulating body that controls the production, supply and marketing of Champagne is CIVC, Comité Interprofessionnel du Vin de Champagne based in Épernay, France.

122) Who is regarded as the 'Father of Champagne'?

Dom Pierre Pérignon.

123) Who was the first to use cork stoppers for Champagne?

Dom Pierre Pérignon.

124) Mention few achievements of Dom Pierre Pérignon.

Dom Pierre Pérignon was the first to make standard quality white wine from black grapes. He mastered the art of blending to create quality wines.

125) For how many years did Dom Pierre Pérignon serve in 'Abbey of Hautvillers' as cellar master?

47 years.

126) Where is 'Abbey of Hautvillers' located at?

Valley of the Marne.

127) Name the only winery in the world where one can view the statue of 'Father of Champagne.'

At the headquarters of Moët & Chandon winery located at Épernay, France.

128) Name the Champagne house from which Moët & Chandon group purchased the legal rights to use the name 'Dom Perignon.'

Mercier.

129) Name few widows better known as Champagne widows who contributed for improving the quality and availability of Champagne.

Madame Veuve Clicquot, Madame Lily Bollinger, Madame Veuve Pommery, Madame Laurent-Perrier etc.

130) Name the woman who won the title 'Grand dame of Champagne.'

Madame Veuve Clicquot.

131) Name the award initiated by Veuve Clicquot Champagne house from the year 1972 to honour the spirit of woman entrepreneurs.

Veuve Clicquot Business Woman Award.

132) Name the stainless steel wine cellar tower designed by Porsche Design Studio for Veuve Clicquot Champagne house.

Vertical Limit.

133) Name an eco-friendly Champagne brand launched by Pommery Champagne house.

POP Earth.

134) "It's not just France we are fighting for, it's Champagne!" Which famous political personality made the above mentioned statement?

Winston Churchill.

135) Which Champagne brand was Sir Winston Churchill's favourite?

Pol Roger.

136) Name the largest independent family owned Champagne house in the world.

Louis Roederer.

137) The smaller the bubbles of Champagne the better the wine- True or False.

True.

138) Name the world's first Champagne house (as per records).

Ruinart started by Nicolas Ruinart in the year 1729.

139) Name the Champagne house which is considered as the 'Giant in Champagne Industry.'

Möet & Chandon.

140) Name three Champagne brands that have been prominent in James Bond movies.

Dom Perignon, Taittinger and the latest one being Bollinger.

141) What's the significance of two letters, 'R.D' mentioned on the label of a Champagne bottle?

It indicates that the wine was 'Recently Disgorged.'

142) What's the term used to denote the large sized bubbles seen in a bottle of Champagne?

'Yeux de crapaud' or Toad's eyes.

143) Give the term used to denote the largest size of Champagne bottle.

Melchizedek or Midas (30 litres capacity, 40 regular sized bottles).

144) What's the term used to denote a band of Champagne bubbles clinging to the sides of a glass?

Collerette.

145) What is the common term used to denote bubbles floating together in a glass of Champagne?

Bead.

146) What is Kosher Champagne?

Champagne made by Jews according to the Jewish dietary laws of 'Kashrut' is termed as Kosher Champagne.

147) Give two brand names for Kosher Champagne.

Laurent Perrier Brut Champagne and Herzog Selection Blanc de Blancs Champagne.

148) Name one Champagne brand that does not feature punt on its bottle.

Cristal.

149) Name the Champagne brand which was made for Russian Tsar, Alexander II.

Cristal.

150) Name two Champagne producers that produce only Vintage Champagne.

Cristal and Salon.

151) Name the Hollywood star who is believed to have bathed in Champagne.

Marilyn Monroe.

152) What is Sabrage?

The act of breaking a Champagne bottle with the help of a saber is termed as Sabrage.

153) Name one of the Champagne houses that age Champagne in ocean.

M.Hostomme.

154) Give examples for Crèmant.

Crèmant d'Alsace, Crèmant de Bourgogne and Crèmant de Loire.

155) What is the disadvantage of Methode Gazifie?

When the fizzy wine is served, the bubbles escape quickly.

156) Who named the different sizes of champagne bottle?

It is believed that the British wine merchants named the champagne bottles between 1850s and 1860s.

157) What is Champagne cascade/tower?

Champagne cascade is a beautiful display of champagne coupe glassware with champagne placed on tiers.

158) Why sparkling wines should be consumed in a tall and narrow glassware?

It is preferred since such glasses can hold the bubbles for longer time. It concentrates the aroma of wine too.

159) Which is the ideal glassware for serving Champagne?

Champagne flute or Champagne tulip since these glasses can hold the bubbles for longer time.

160) Give five brand names of Champagne.

Moët & Chandon, Ayala, Lanson, Krug and Taittinger.

161) Name few sparkling wines from other regions of France.

Vouvray Mousseux (Loire region of France), Saumur Mousseux (Commune of Saumur) and Crémant d'Alsace (Alsace region of France).

162) Name three glassware used to serve sparkling wines.

Champagne flute, Champagne tulip and Champagne saucer.

163) Name India's first sparkling wine.

Marquise de Pompadour/Omar Khayyam.

164) Which is India's first sparkling wine brand to feature gold flakes in the bottle?

Grover Zampa's Auriga.

165) Name Möet & Chandon group's Indian sparkling wine brand.

Chandon.

166) Which is India's first sparkling wine based on Shiraz grape variety?

Sula Sparkling Shiraz.

167) Name India's first 'Blanc de blanc' sparkling wine.

York Sparkling Cuvée made from 100% Chenin blanc.

168) Give four brand names of Indian sparkling wines.

York Sparkling Cuvée, Chandon Brut, Sula Brut and Vinsura Brut.

169) Which Champagne house produced 'Champagne Marilyn Monroe Premier Cru Brut' to commemorate the 50th death anniversary of the famous Hollywood actress, Marilyn Monroe?

JM Gobillard & Fils

170) What is Sekt?

Sekt is a sparkling wine that hails from Austria and Germany.

171) When is 'Austrian Sekt Day' celebrated?

'Austrian Sekt Day' is celebrated every year on 22nd of October.

172) Name the governing body that sets the standards for Austrian Sekt.

Sekt g.U

173) Name the three categories of Austrian Sekt.

Grosse Reserve, Reserve and Klassik.

174) What are Grosse Reserve wines?

These are top quality Austrian Sekts which are made from grapes harvested and pressed in a single municipality and then traditionally fermented in bottles. The wine should mature on lees for at least a minimum period of 30 months.

175) What are Reserve Sekts?

Sekts that is less superior to Grosse Reserve wines are termed as Reserve Sekts. Such kinds of wines are matured on lees for a minimum period of 18 months.

176) What are Klassik Sekts?

Klassik Sekts could follow any methods to add sparkle to the wine. All the grapes harvested for making this wine should come from one Austrian Federal State.

177) What is Sektglas Österreich?

Sektglass Austria is a special type of glassware designed to serve various styles of Austrian Sekt.

178) Give two brand names of Spanish Cava.

Freixenet Sparkling Cordon Negro and Anna de Codorniu.

179) What is the bottom indentation of a sparkling wine bottle called?

Punt.

180) Why there is a punt in the bottom of certain wine bottles?

It helps to collect sediments present in wine and enables the wine waiters to hold the bottle in the right manner. In the case of sparkling wines, the bottom indentation aids in even distribution of pressure created by carbon dioxide present in the bottle.

181) Why we hear a 'pop' sound while opening a sparkling wine bottle?

This happens as the pressure inside the bottle is let out.

182) What are Fortified wines/Dessert wines/Vins de liqueur?

Fortified wines are those wines to which brandy (distilled grape spirit) is added to increase the alcoholic content.

183) What is Muted wine/Vins mutes?

Wine to which brandy is added either to halt the fermentation process or to increase the alcoholic content is termed as Muted wine.

184) What is fortification?

Fortification is a term used to denote the process of adding brandy to wine.

185) Give few examples for Fortified wines

Sherry (Southern Spain), **Port** (Northern Portugal), **Madeira** (Madeira), **Marsala** (Sicily) and **Malaga** (*Málaga).*

186) What is Sherry?

Sherry is a fortified wine made by the fractional blending process with an alcoholic content of 16 to 22%.

187) What is the old name of Sherry wine?

Sack.

188) What is 'flor' in relation to Sherry?

Flor is a layer of yeast which might or might not form on top of the Sherry wine. If formed, flor develops a veil (velo de flor) on top of the wine (looks like froth).

189) Explain the role of 'flor' in Sherry wine.

Flor, a layer of yeast prevents air from entering the Sherry wine thereby protecting the wine from oxidation. Flor also seals the wine from harmful bacteria and gives flavour to the wine.

190) Name the yeasts present in 'flor.'

Flor comprises of four yeasts namely sacchromyces beticus, sacchromyces montuliensis, sacchromyces cheresiensis and sacchromyces rouxii.

191) What is Solera System of Sherry?

Solera system is a famous blending and maturing technique adopted for making Sherry. Solera system comprises of a group of casks (butts) placed one on top of the other in a bodegas (wine cellar/store room). The oldest wines are always stored in the bottom casks and the youngest ones on top. The wine required for sales is partially drawn from the bottom casks.

192) What is the meaning of the word 'solera'?

It means 'casks touching the ground.'

193) In a solera system, what does the term 'solera' mean?

The final row (bottom row) of criadera (casks) in the solera system is known as 'Solera'

194) Name the different types of Sherry.

Fino, Manzanilla, Amontillado, Oloroso and Cream sherry.

195) What is Fino Sherry?

Fino Sherry is a type of sherry which is developed with the aid of flor (yeast like fungus).The alcohol content is almost 15% and is the driest among all styles of Sherry.

196) What is Manzanilla?

Manzanilla is a type of fino sherry which is dry in nature with 15% alcohol content. The flavour of the wine resembles that of chamomile tea and hence the name. Though Manzanilla sherry is made in a similar fashion to that of Fino, it is made from grapes grown by the sea at Sanlùcar de Barrameda.

197) What is Amontillado Sherry?

Answer- Another version of Fino sherry which is named after the Montilla region of Spain is Amontillado. It is full bodied, has got alcoholic level varying between 16 to 18%.

198) What is Oloroso?

Oloroso is a type of sherry which appears naturally dry and is used as the base for making sweet sherries.

199) What is Cream Sherry?

A very popular style of sherry is Cream sherry. It could be sweetened Amontillado or Oloroso. This full bodied style of sherry is sweet and dark in colour. Cream sherry is an after dinner drink and goes really well with coffee.

200) Give few brand names of Sherry wine.

Sandeman, Harveys, Garvey, Croft and Osborne.

201) Where Sherry is produced in Spain?

Sherry is produced in Jerez de la Frontera in Andalusia, Spain.

202) What is ABV and TCA?

ABV stands for Alcohol By Volume and TCA stands for Trichloro anisole.

203) What is Port/Vinho do Porto/Vin de Porto?

Port is a classic fortified dessert wine manufactured in Upper Douro valley of Portugal with alcoholic content ranging between 18 to 22%.

204) Who invented Port wine?

British wine merchants.

205) How can you identify an original bottle of port wine?

The real port wine from Portugal bears the name 'Porto' on its wine label.

206) How port wine got its name?

The name Port has been derived from the city of Oporto located at the mouth of the Douro River.

207) What is Lagar/Lagares?

Lagares are granite troughs approximately 3-6 m across and 60 cm deep which is used for crushing grapes by foot treading. The workers used to remove their shoes and socks, roll up their trousers and systematically march back and forth over the grapes.

208) Name the sail boats used to transport port wine down river to Oporto for maturation and aging.

Barcos rabelos.

209) Name the special building in which the blending and aging process of port wine takes place.

Lodges.

210) Name the large, lengthy barrels with tapered ends used for aging port wine.

Pipes.

211) Which are the two types of port?

Bottle aged ports and Wood aged ports.

212) What is Port tongs?

Port tongs is a special wine equipment used for opening Vintage port bottles.

213) Name few brand names of Port wine.

Dow, Sandeman, Taylor, Graham and Ferreira.

214) Name the 'World's most indestructible wine.'

Madeira wine from the island of Madeira, Portugal.

215) Name the only wine in the world which is baked.

Madeira wine.

216) What is Estufa system/Estufagem?

The process of heating or cooking Madeira wine in estufas for acquiring flavour as well as increasing the longevity of the wine is termed as Estufa system.

217) Name few brand names of Madeira wine.

Leacock's, Blandy's, Sandeman, Justino and Miles.

218) Name few elements that can affect wine.

Light (affects the colour of the wine), **heat** (wine oxidises prematurely), **vibrations** (it might stir up the sediments present in the wine) and **temperature fluctuations**.

219) What is the ideal temperature for storing wine?

The ideal temperature for storing wine is between 10°C-13°C.

220) Where wine could be stored?

Wine cellar, wine racks, wine refrigerators and cabinets.

221) What is wine cellar?

A wine cellar is an ideal store room in which wines could be stored in bottles as well as barrels. Good wine cellars feature wine racks and are normally located underground since wine need to be stored in low temperature.

222) What are wine racks?

Wine racks are primarily designed to hold wine bottles in a wine cellar.

223) Why wine bottles sealed with cork should be stored horizontally?

Glass wine bottles sealed with corks must be stored on their side (laid horizontally) so that the wine is in contact with the cork. This action ensures that the cork is moist all the time and the cork do not let in too much air.

224) Give the right kind of glassware used in the service of wine.

Wine	Glassware
White	White wine glass
Red	Red wine glass and Paris goblet
Rosé	White wine glass
Champagne & other sparkling wines	Champagne flute or tulip glassware
Port	Port dock glassware
Sherry	Sherry copita or Elgin shaped sherry glassware

225) Give the right serving temperature of table, sparkling and fortified wines.

Wine	Serving temperature
White	9-14°C
Red	13-20°C
Rosé	7-13 °C
Champagne & other sparkling wines	6-8°C
Fortified wines	13-20 °C

226) What is Decanting?

Decanting is a process of transferring wine from its original bottle to the decanter with the motive of removing sediments from the wine.

227) Why decanting process is carried out?

Decanting benefits the wine in the following ways-

- ✓ Allows the wine to breathe

- ✓ Wine develops bouquet

- ✓ Sediments get totally separated from the wine.

228) How the sediments occur in aged wines?

These sediments are natural deposits of tannins and other colour pigments present in the wine that have developed over years.

229) Name the equipments required for the decanting process.

A clean decanter, decanting funnel/muslin cloth and a light source (normally candle).

230) Give any five points related to wine and food harmony.

- ✓ Balance the weight of the food with the weight of the wine

- ✓ Serve dry wines before sweet wines

- ✓ Food from a particular region will often match a type of wine from the same region

- ✓ National dishes should be complemented by the national wines of that country (E.g.-Italian Chianti with pizza)

- ✓ If a particular wine is used in the preparation of a dish, use the same wine to drink with the dish.

231) Name few defects/faults of wine

Oxidised wine, cloudiness in wine, corked wine, wine diamonds and weeping of wines.

232) What are Wine diamonds/ Crystalline deposits?

They are generally seen either at the bottom of the bottle or at the bottom of the cork. Crystalline deposits are basically tasteless potassium bitartrate and normally occur when wine is exposed to low temperature.

233) What is 'Weeping of wines'?

This fault is often seen when the wine bottles are kept for storing. Wine seeps out of the bottle through the sides of the cork thereby reducing the quantity of wine in the bottle. It could either occur due to a faulty cork or secondary fermentation happening inside the bottle (pushes the cork and makes it loose).

234) What are 'tears of wine'?

This happens when a glass of wine is swirled. Once the swirling is stopped, one can witness wine droplets clinging to the sides of the glass moving down to the bottom. This phenomenon is also referred to as 'legs' of wine.

235) What is an Apéritif?

An Apéritif is any alcoholic drink served before a meal which is intended to increase the appetite of the consumer.

236) What is the nature of Apéritifs?

Apéritifs are alcoholic drinks which are generally dry and sometimes spicy too. They are mostly served cold.

237) What is the meaning of the word Apéritif?

Apéritif is derived from the Latin word 'aperire' which means 'to open'.

238) Name few wine aperitifs.

Sparkling wines, especially the ones that are bone dry, White wines (dry), Sherry (dry), Port (dry), Madeira (dry), Blanc de noirs etc.

239) Name few wine apéritif brands

Vermouth, Campari, Lillet, Dubonnet, Pernod, St.Raphaël etc.

240) What are Digestifs?

Digestifs are alcoholic beverages that are consumed at the end of a meal.

241) Give examples for aromatized wines

Vermouth, Dubonnet, Lillet and St.Raphaël.

242) What is Vermouth?

Vermouth is regarded as the world's most famous aromatized wine which could be either served as an apéritif or digestif. It is a normal white wine with an alcoholic content of 16% ABV, slightly fortified (with brandy) and flavoured.

243) What are the various styles of vermouth?

The various styles of vermouth include Dry, Red, Rosé and Flavoured.

244) Give few brand names of Vermouth.

Noilly Prat, Martini, Cinzano, Boissiere and Punt e Mes.

245) What is Dubonnet?

Dubonnet is a wine based apéritif that comes from France. Dubonnet is also produced in United States under license.

246) What are Bitters?

The term 'bitters' cover a wide array of spirits that possess either bitter or bitter sweet taste obtained from numerous roots (e.g.-gentian root) and herbs. Various flavouring agents like seeds, flowers, berries, bark etc. used in bitters are responsible for the final flavour of the bitter.

247) What is Campari?

This famous red coloured bitter apéritif was invented by Gaspare Campari in Milan, Italy. Its secret recipe is said to feature 60 botanical ingredients.

248) What is Angostura bitter?

Angostura bitter is a type of cocktail bitter which was born at Angostura in Venezuela but is currently produced in Trinidad. It is made from a secret blend of herbs and spices.

249) Which are the types of bitters?

Apéritif/ digestif bitters and Cocktail bitters.

250) Give examples for Apéritif/ digestif bitters.

Campari, Cynar, Amer Picon, Fernet Branca and Jägermeister.

251) What is Chaptalisation?

Chaptalisation is the process of adding sugar to the must in order to increase alcoholic content of the final product. This step can be carried out either before the actual fermentation happens or during the fermentation process.

252) What is Malo-lactic fermentation?

Malo-lactic fermentation is secondary fermentation that most wines go through naturally. Here harsh malic acid gets converted into softer lactic acid.

253) What are 'Lees'?

The solid particles including used yeast cells and grape pulp present in the newly made wine starts sinking to the bottom of the casks. These sediments are known as 'Lees'.

254) What is Racking?

The process of transferring wine from one cask to the other or from one tank to the other till it becomes acceptably clear is called Racking.

255) What is Fining?

Fining is a step in vinification by which the suspended bodies that makes wine cloudy is cleared out.

256) What are Fining agents? Give few examples

The agents used in the fining process are termed as Fining agents. Isinglass (bladder of sturgeon fish), Egg whites, Casein, Gelatine, Dried albumen and Bentonite (a type of clay formed by the weathering of volcanic rock) are examples for fining agents.

257) What is the standard circumference of wine cork?

#9.

258) Why corks are used as enclosures for wine bottles?

Corks permit little amount of oxygen to enter the wine bottle. Cork allows the flavour to develop in wine and enables tannins present in wine to mellow down.

259) Why the wine cork is generally sealed?

This is done to keep the contaminants away and to keep bugs away.

260) Why rosé wine bottles does not feature corks?

Rosé wine bottles comes with screw cap as the wine is not aged.

261) What is wine cork made up of?

Wine cork is made from the bark of cork oak tree.

262) Which German wine means 'milk of the blessed mother'?

Liebfraumilch, a semi-sweet white wine.

263) From which country comes Egri Bikaver, bull's blood wine?

Hungary.

264) Which wine is known as the 'Champagne of Italy'?

Franciacorta.

265) Name the grape varietal known as Primitivo in Italy.

Zinfandel.

Bibliography

Lillicrap Dennis, Cousins John and Weekes Suzanne. 2014. *Food and Beverage Service (9th edition.)* United Kingdom. Hodder Education.

Owens Bill, Dikty Alan. 2009. *The Art of Distilling Whiskey and Other Spirits: An Enthusiast's Guide to the Artisan Distilling of Potent Potables.* USA. Quarry Books.

Foskett David, Rippington Neil, Paskins Patricia, Thorpe Steve. 2015. *Practical Cookery (13th edition.)* United Kingdom. Hodder Education.

DeLove L.Chandler. *2004. Bartending for the Professional and Home Entertainer.* USA. American Book Company.

Williams Olivia. 2014. *Gin Glorious Gin: How Mother's Ruin Became the Spirit of London* London. Headline Publishing Group.

Belair-Liger Gérard. 2013. *Uncorked: The Science of Champagne.* New Jersey. Princeton University Press.

The following websites were accessed during January 2021-May 2021)

https://www.vegrecipesofindia.com/gulab-jamun-recipe-with-khoya/

https://lancaster.unl.edu/enviro/water/ww10_04.shtml

http://www.belgiangenever.com/about-belgian-genever.html

http://www.ginfoundry.com/gin/plymouth-gin/

https://globaltea.ucdavis.edu/all-about-tea

http://www.champagneguide.net/information/glossary

https://recipes.timesofindia.com/articles/food-facts/revealed-the-secret-behind-these-7-popular-indian-food-traditions/photostory/61658949.cms